THE STORY OF MICHAEL JACKSON

KING OF POP

BY TERRY COLLINS

ILLUSTRATED BY MICHAEL BYERS

Content Consultant:
Meredith E. Rutledge, Assistant Curator
Rock and Roll Hall of Fame and Museum
Cleveland, Ohio

CAPSTONE PRESS
a capstone imprint

Graphic Library is published by Capstone Press,

1710 Roe Crest Drive
North Mankato, MN 56003

www.capstonepub.com

Books published by Capstone Press are
manufactured with paper containing at least
10 percent post-consumer waste.

Library of Congress Cataloging-in-Publication Data

Collins, Terry (Terry Carlson)
      King of pop : the story of Michael Jackson/
by Terry Collins.
      p. cm. — (Graphic library. American graphic)
      Includes bibliographical references and index.
      Summary: "Describes important moments and
accomplishments in Michael Jackson's life in graphic novel
format"—Provided by publisher.
      ISBN 978-1-4296-6015-0 (library binding)
      ISBN 978-1-4296-7994-7 (paperback)
      1. Jackson, Michael, 1958–2009—Juvenile
literature. 2. Rock musicians—United States—
Biography—Juvenile literature. 3. Jackson, Michael,
1958–2009—Comic books, strips, etc. 4. Rock
musicians—United States—Biography—Comic books,
strips, etc. I. Title.
ML3930.J25C65 2012
782.42166092—dc23 [B]   2011034673

Printed in the United States of America in
Stevens Point, Wisconsin.

102011   006404WZS12

Direct quotations appear in orange on the following
pages:

Pages 7, 10, 11, 13, 17, 18, 19, 23, from *Michael
Jackson: The Magic, the Madness, the Whole Story,
1958–2009* by J. Randy Taraborrelli (New York: Grand
Central Publishing, 2009).

Page 14, from "Michael Jackson's Life & Legacy: Global
Superstar (1982-86)." VH1

Page 26, from *People* magazine online. Tuesday, July
07, 2009.

Photo Credit
Corbis: Bettmann, 28

Artistic Effect
Shutterstock: kaspri (vivyl record)

Art Director: Nathan Gassman

Editor: Mandy Robbins

Production Specialist: Laura Manthe

Chapter 1
MAN IN THE MIRROR

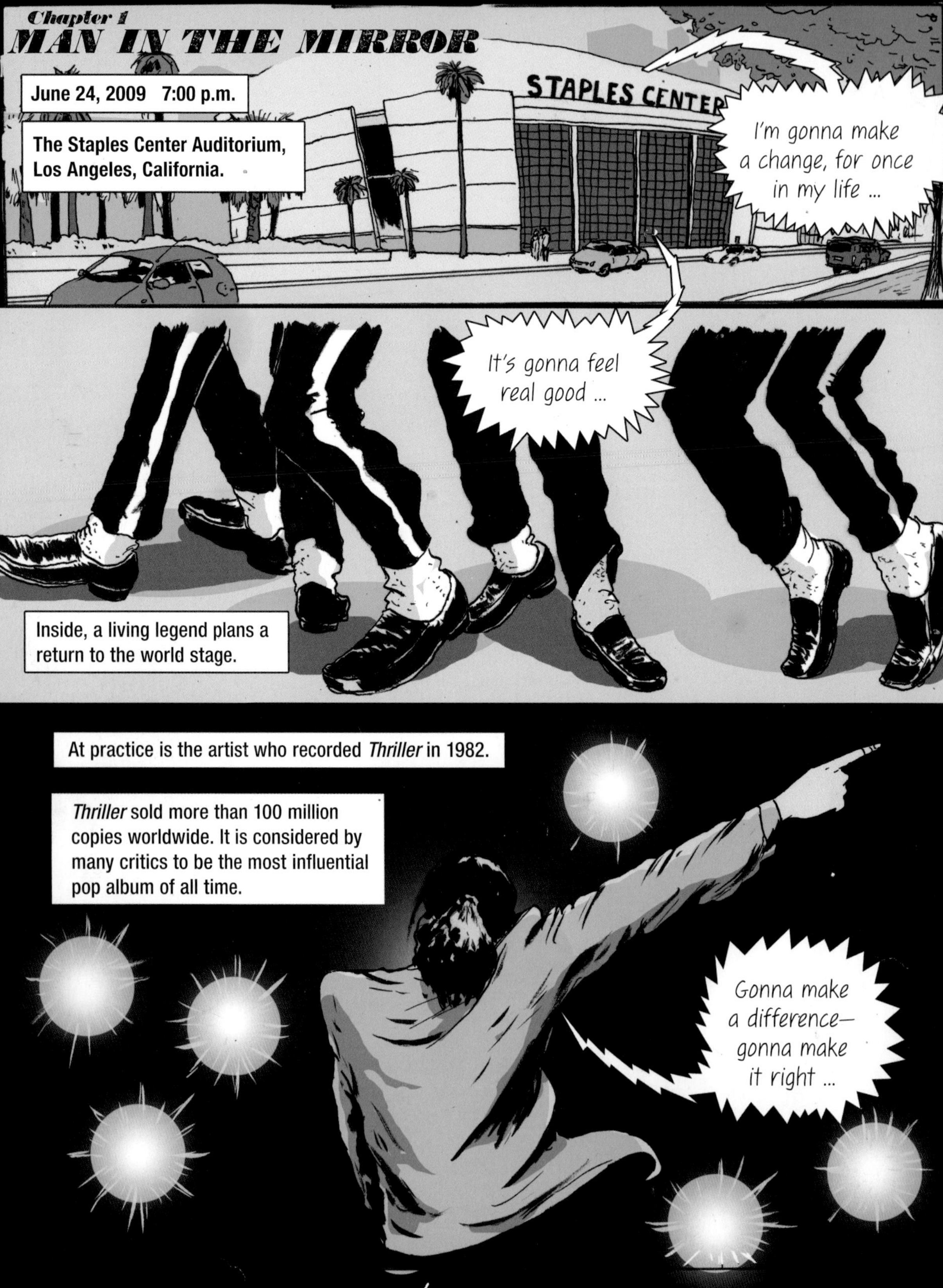
June 24, 2009 7:00 p.m.
The Staples Center Auditorium, Los Angeles, California.
STAPLES CENTER
I'm gonna make a change, for once in my life ...
It's gonna feel real good ...
Inside, a living legend plans a return to the world stage.
At practice is the artist who recorded *Thriller* in 1982.
Thriller sold more than 100 million copies worldwide. It is considered by many critics to be the most influential pop album of all time.
Gonna make a difference— gonna make it right ...

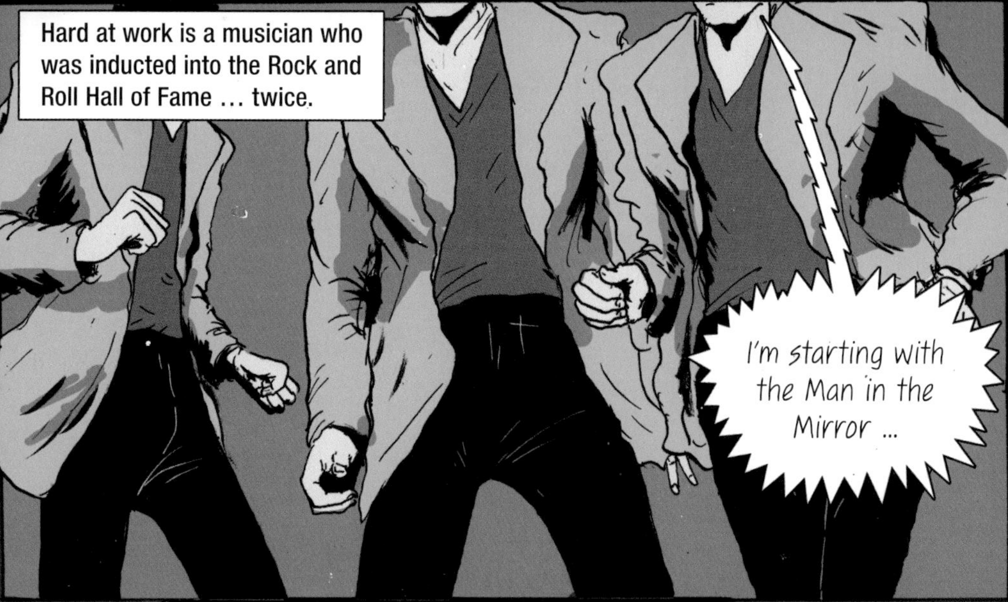
Hard at work is a musician who was inducted into the Rock and Roll Hall of Fame … twice.
I'm starting with the Man in the Mirror …

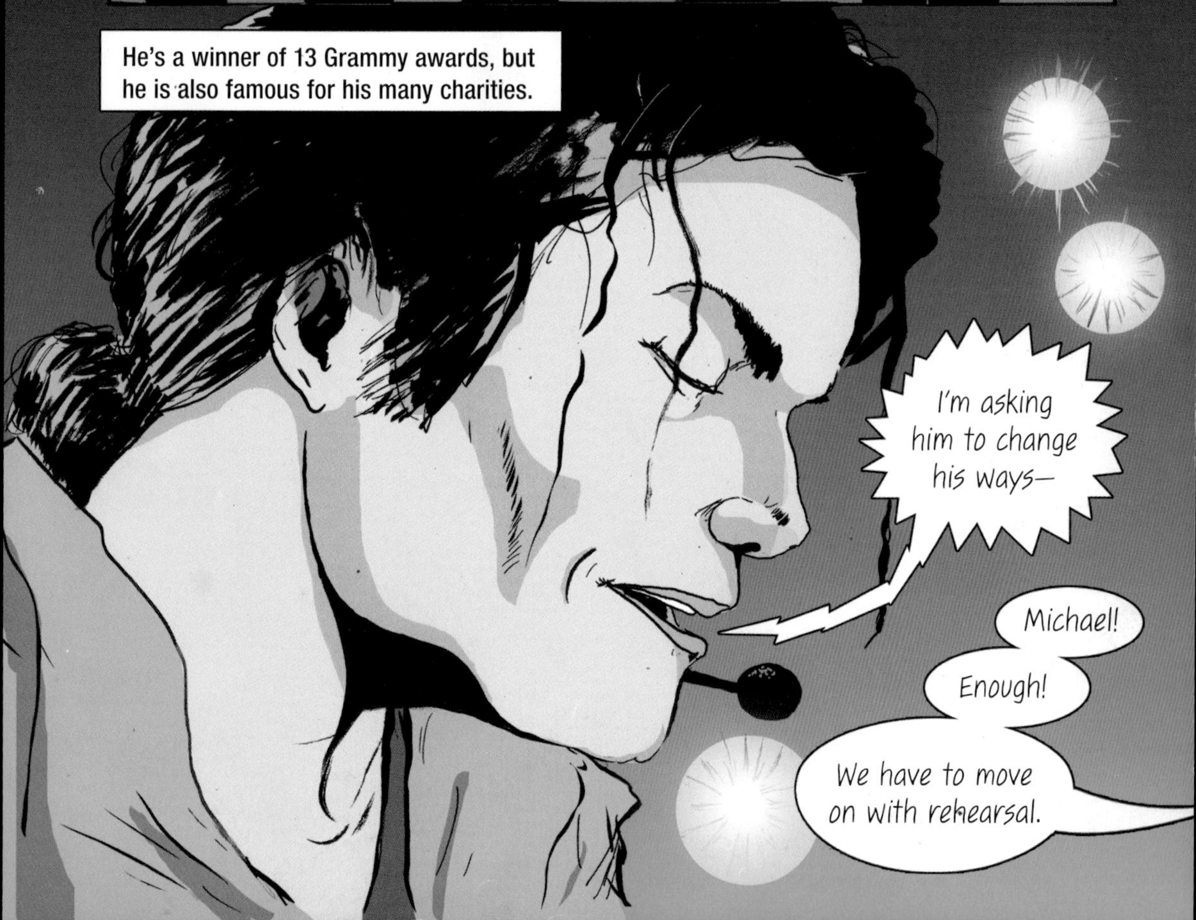
He's a winner of 13 Grammy awards, but he is also famous for his many charities.
I'm asking him to change his ways—
Michael!
Enough!
We have to move on with rehearsal.

Chapter 2
REMEMBER THE TIME

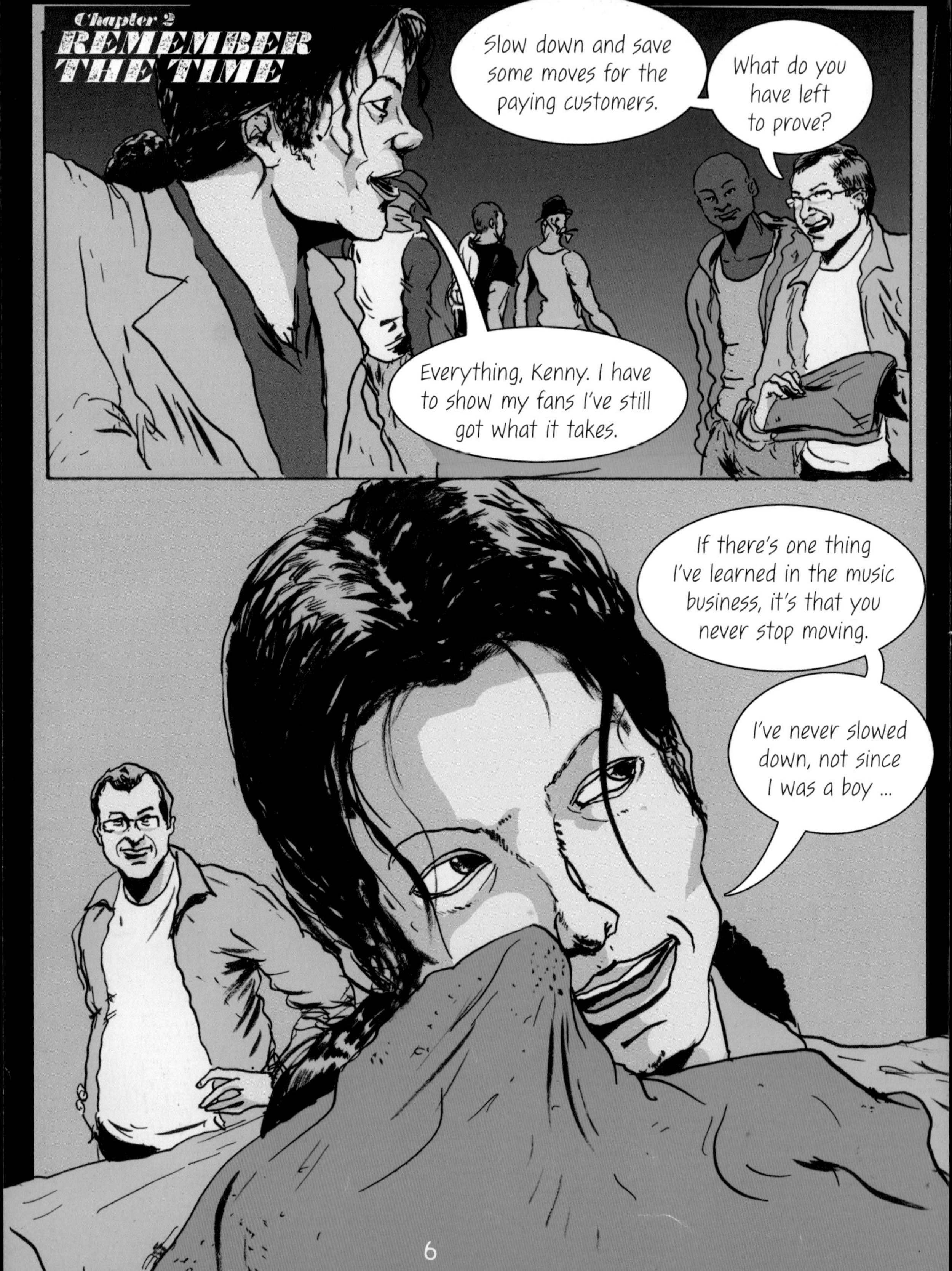
Slow down and save some moves for the paying customers.
What do you have left to prove?
Everything, Kenny. I have to show my fans I've still got what it takes.
If there's one thing I've learned in the music business, it's that you never stop moving.
I've never slowed down, not since I was a boy ...

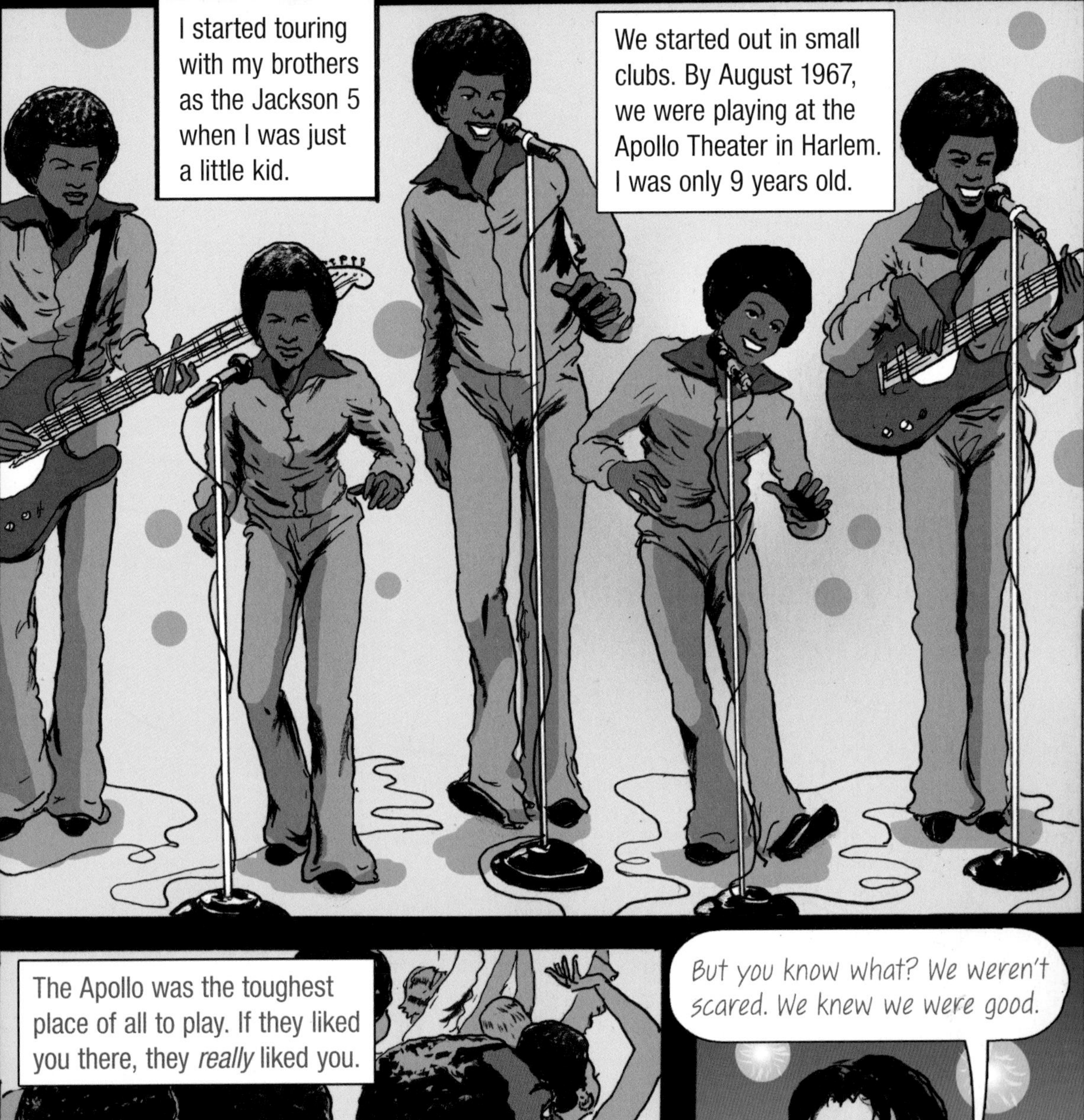
I started touring with my brothers as the Jackson 5 when I was just a little kid.
We started out in small clubs. By August 1967, we were playing at the Apollo Theater in Harlem. I was only 9 years old.

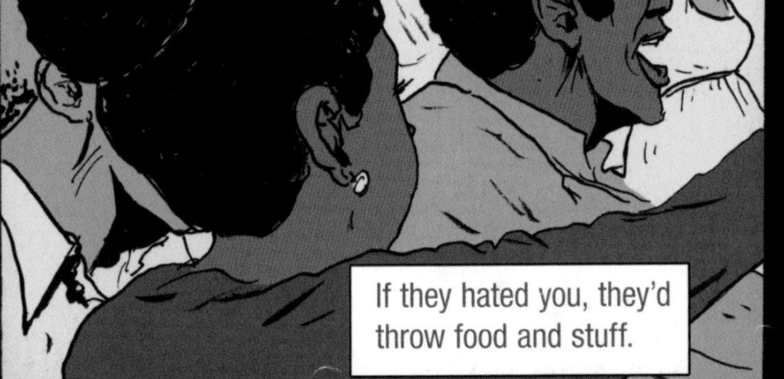
The Apollo was the toughest place of all to play. If they liked you there, they *really* liked you.
If they hated you, they'd throw food and stuff.

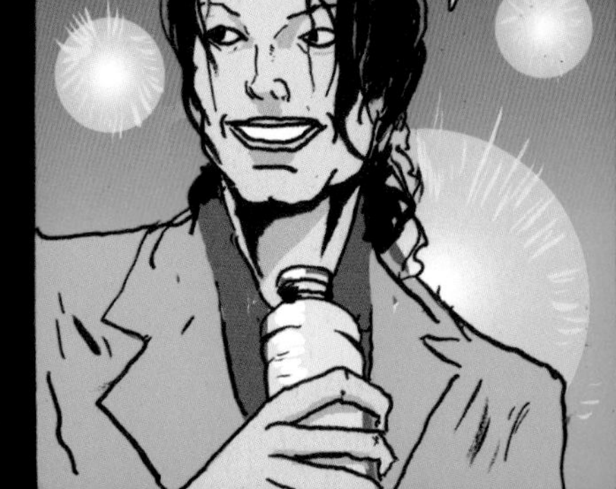
But you know what? We weren't scared. We knew we were good.

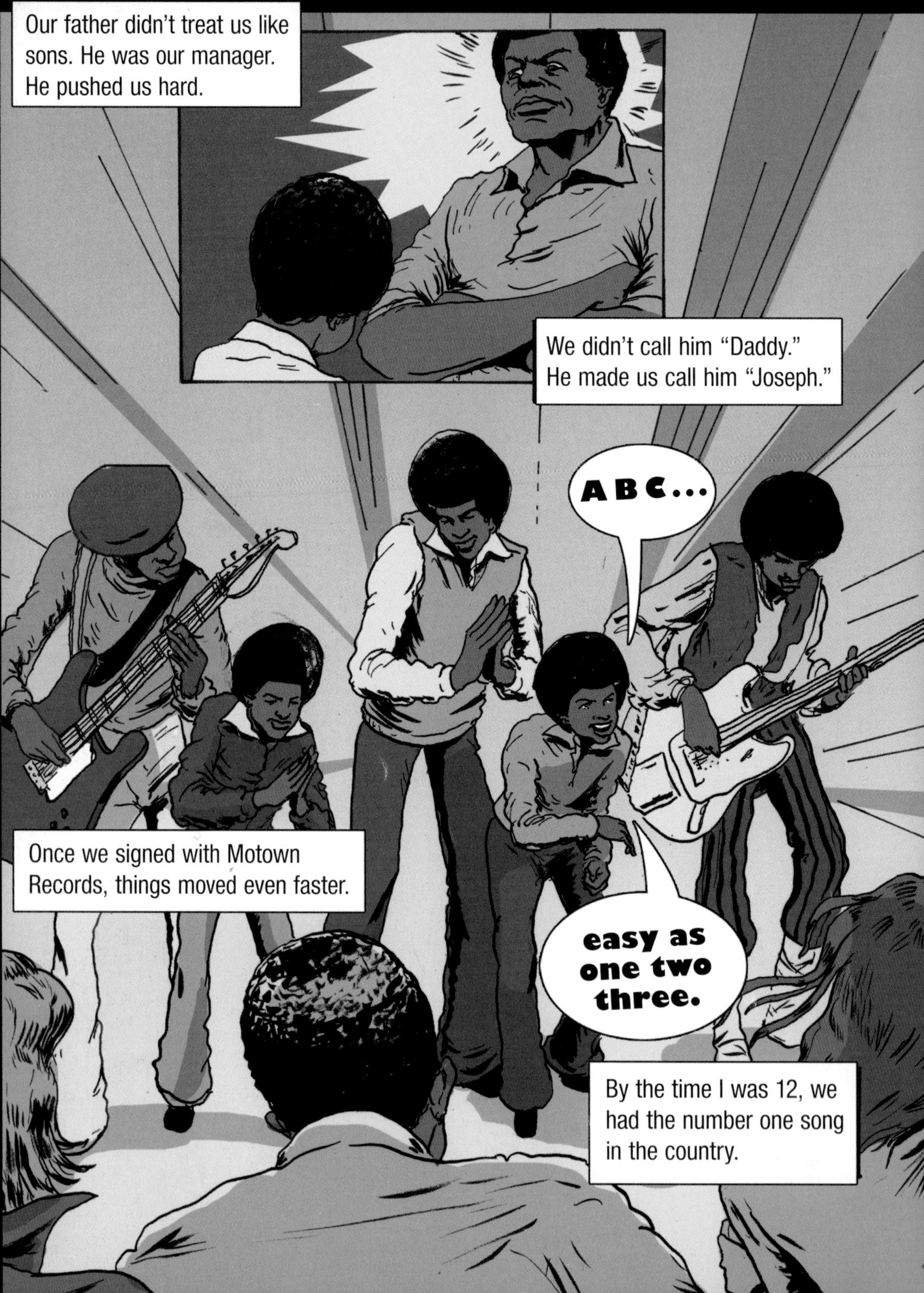

Our father didn't treat us like sons. He was our manager. He pushed us hard.
We didn't call him "Daddy." He made us call him "Joseph."
ABC...
Once we signed with Motown Records, things moved even faster.
easy as one two three.
By the time I was 12, we had the number one song in the country.

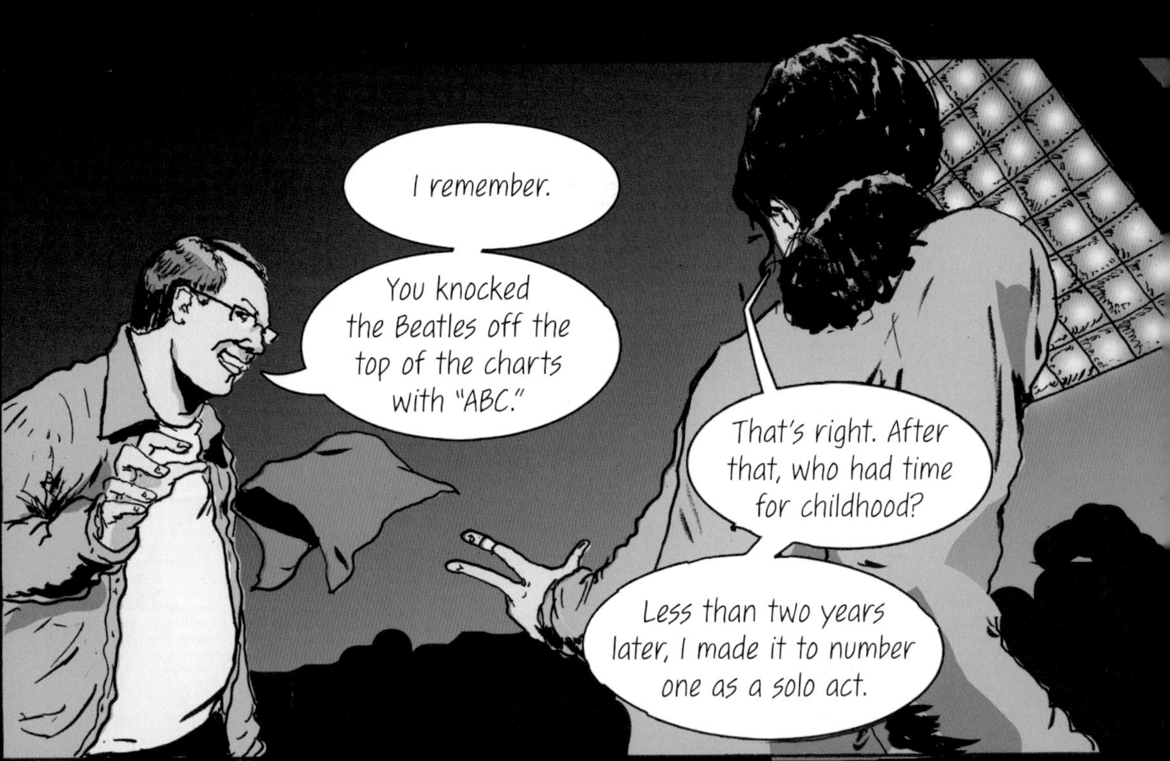
I remember.
You knocked the Beatles off the top of the charts with "ABC."
That's right. After that, who had time for childhood?
Less than two years later, I made it to number one as a solo act.

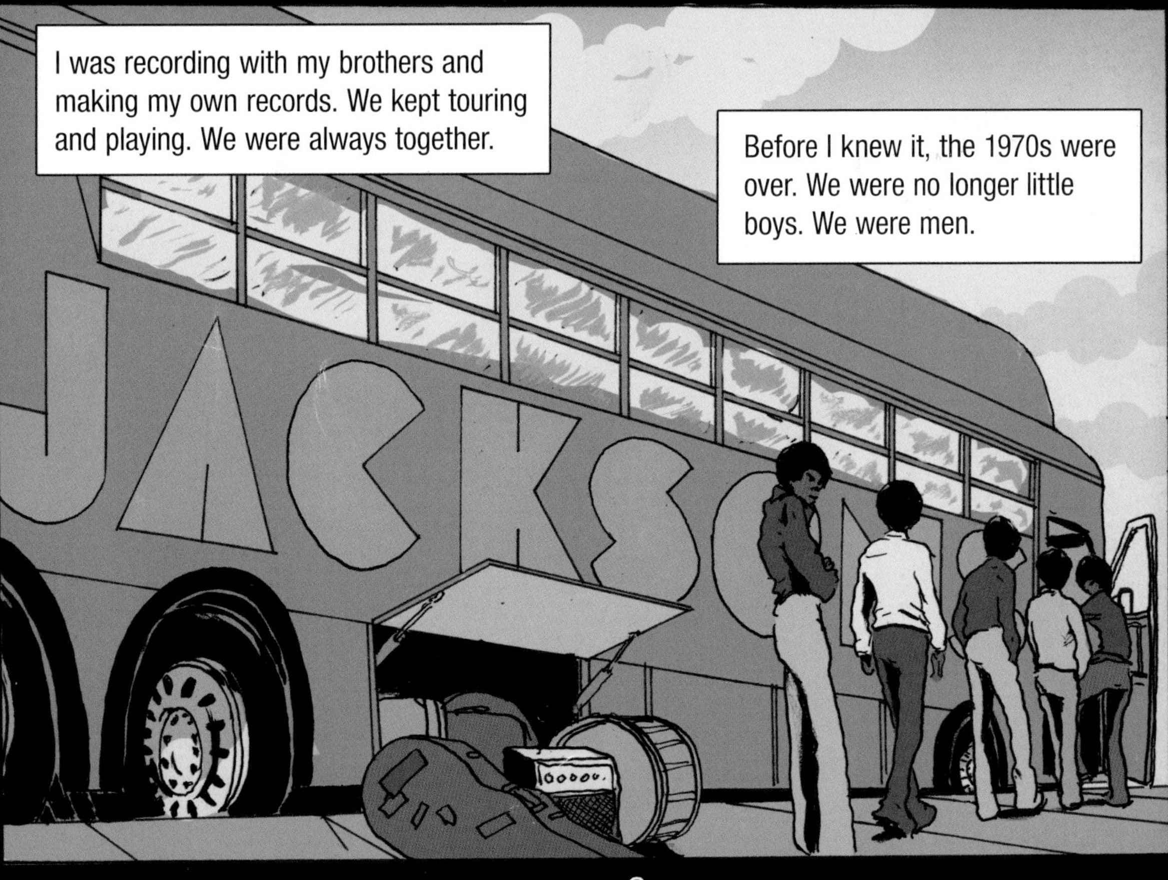
I was recording with my brothers and making my own records. We kept touring and playing. We were always together.
Before I knew it, the 1970s were over. We were no longer little boys. We were men.
JACKSO

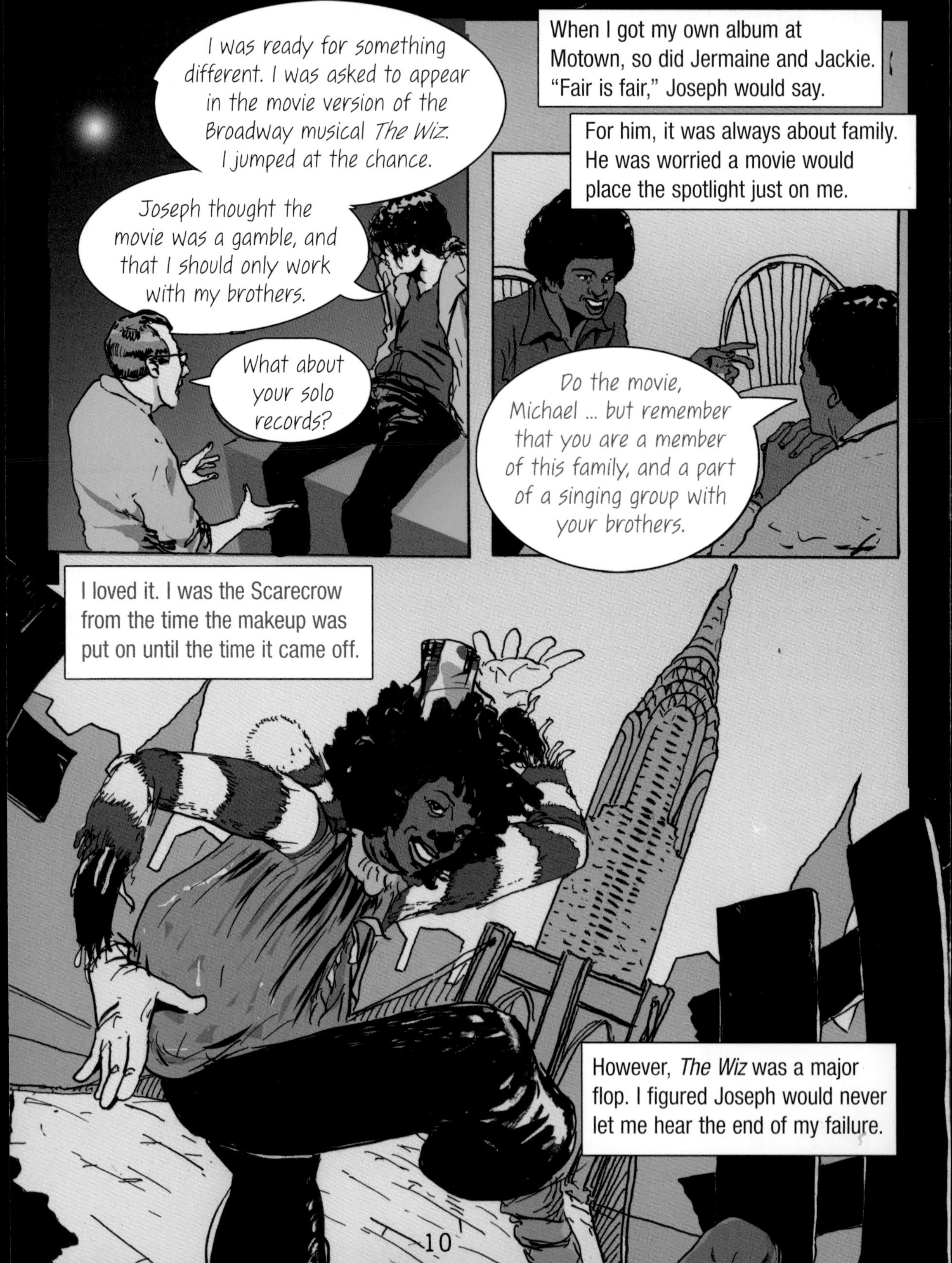
I was ready for something different. I was asked to appear in the movie version of the Broadway musical *The Wiz.* I jumped at the chance.
Joseph thought the movie was a gamble, and that I should only work with my brothers.
What about your solo records?
When I got my own album at Motown, so did Jermaine and Jackie. "Fair is fair," Joseph would say.
For him, it was always about family. He was worried a movie would place the spotlight just on me.
Do the movie, Michael ... but remember that you are a member of this family, and a part of a singing group with your brothers.
I loved it. I was the Scarecrow from the time the makeup was put on until the time it came off.
However, *The Wiz* was a major flop. I figured Joseph would never let me hear the end of my failure.

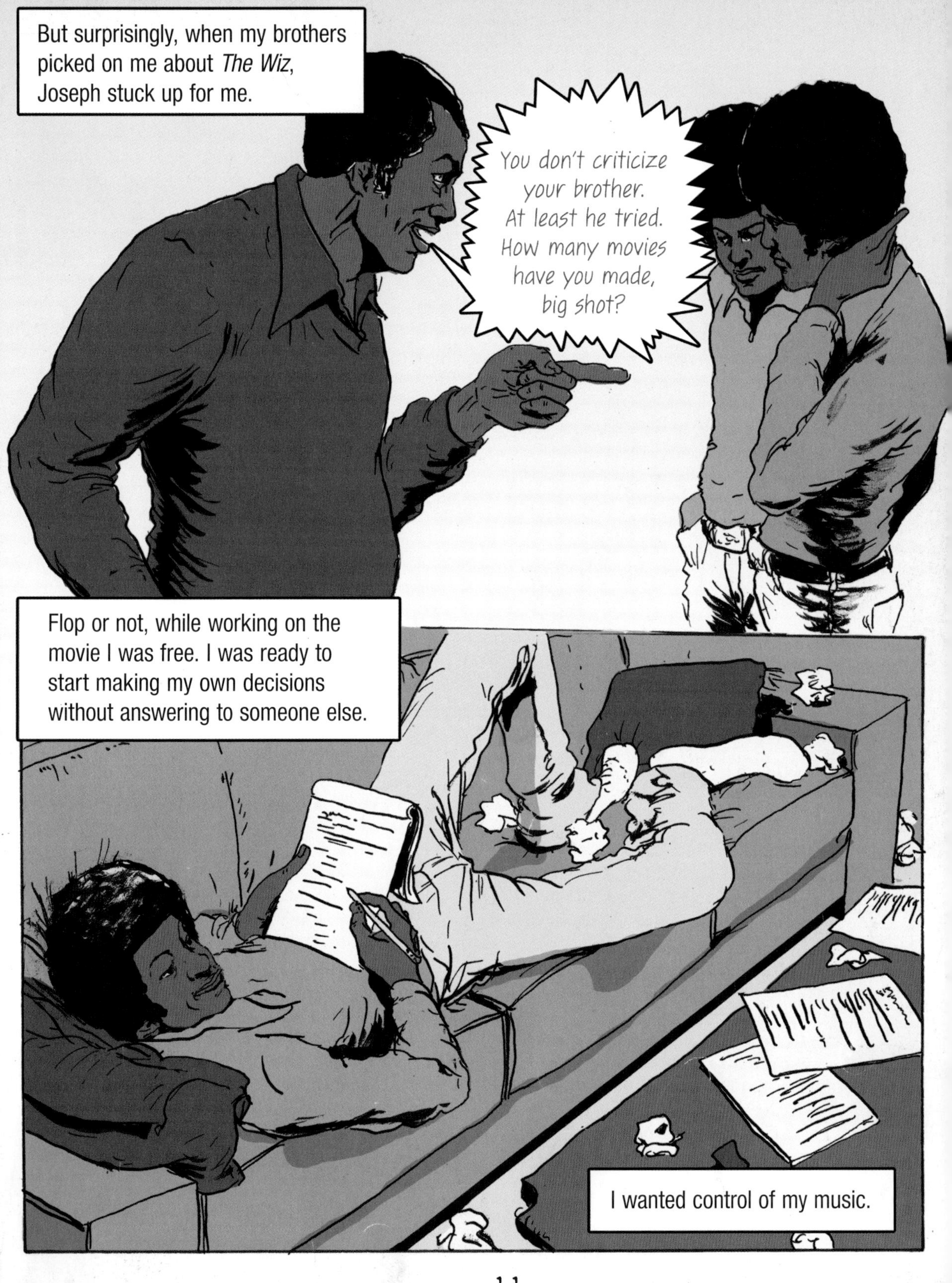

But surprisingly, when my brothers picked on me about *The Wiz*, Joseph stuck up for me.
You don't criticize your brother. At least he tried. How many movies have you made, big shot?
Flop or not, while working on the movie I was free. I was ready to start making my own decisions without answering to someone else.
I wanted control of my music.

Chapter 3

DON'T STOP 'TIL YOU GET ENOUGH

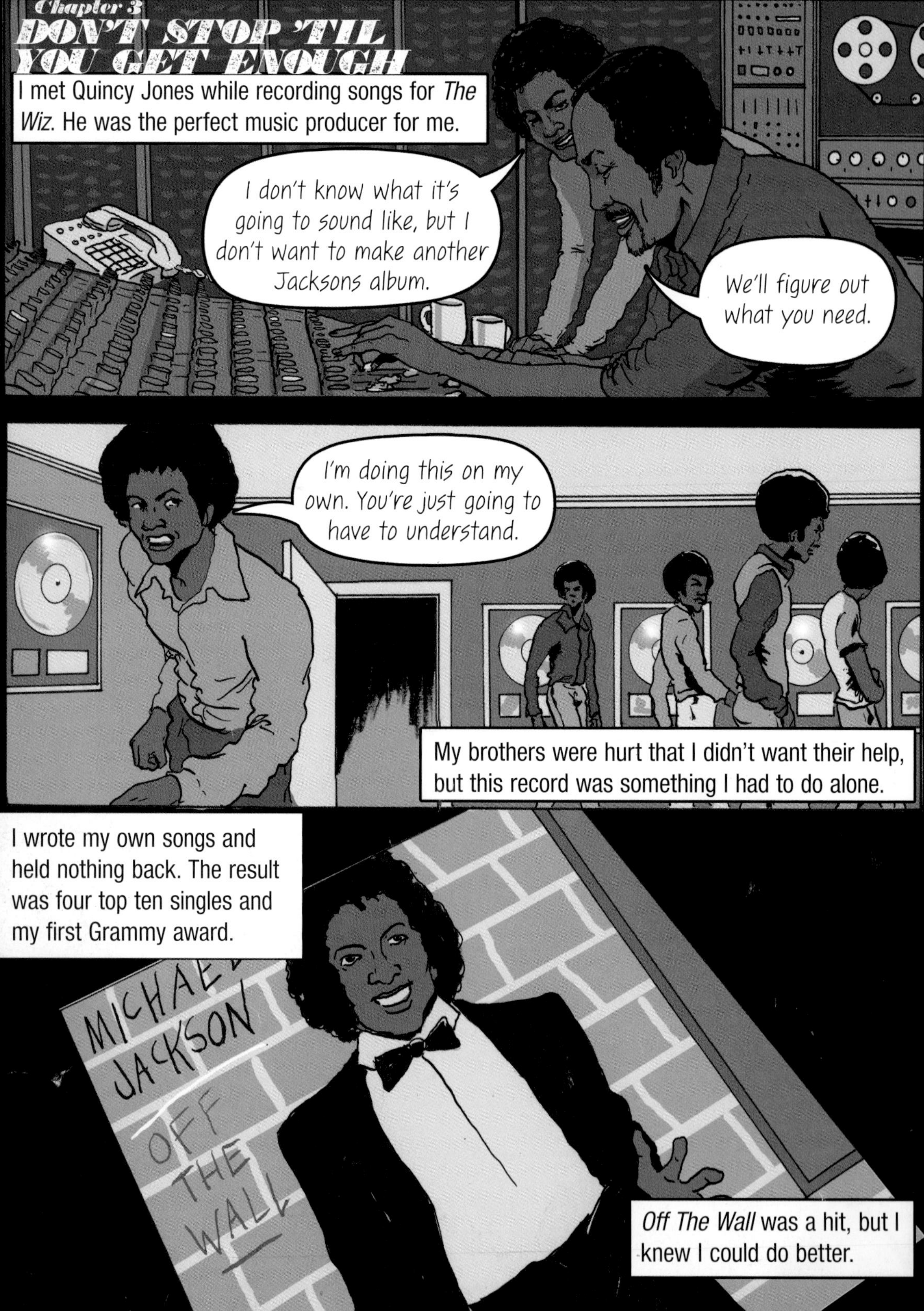
I met Quincy Jones while recording songs for *The Wiz*. He was the perfect music producer for me.
I don't know what it's going to sound like, but I don't want to make another Jacksons album.
We'll figure out what you need.
I'm doing this on my own. You're just going to have to understand.
My brothers were hurt that I didn't want their help, but this record was something I had to do alone.
I wrote my own songs and held nothing back. The result was four top ten singles and my first Grammy award.
MICHAEL JACKSON
OFF THE WALL
Off The Wall was a hit, but I knew I could do better.

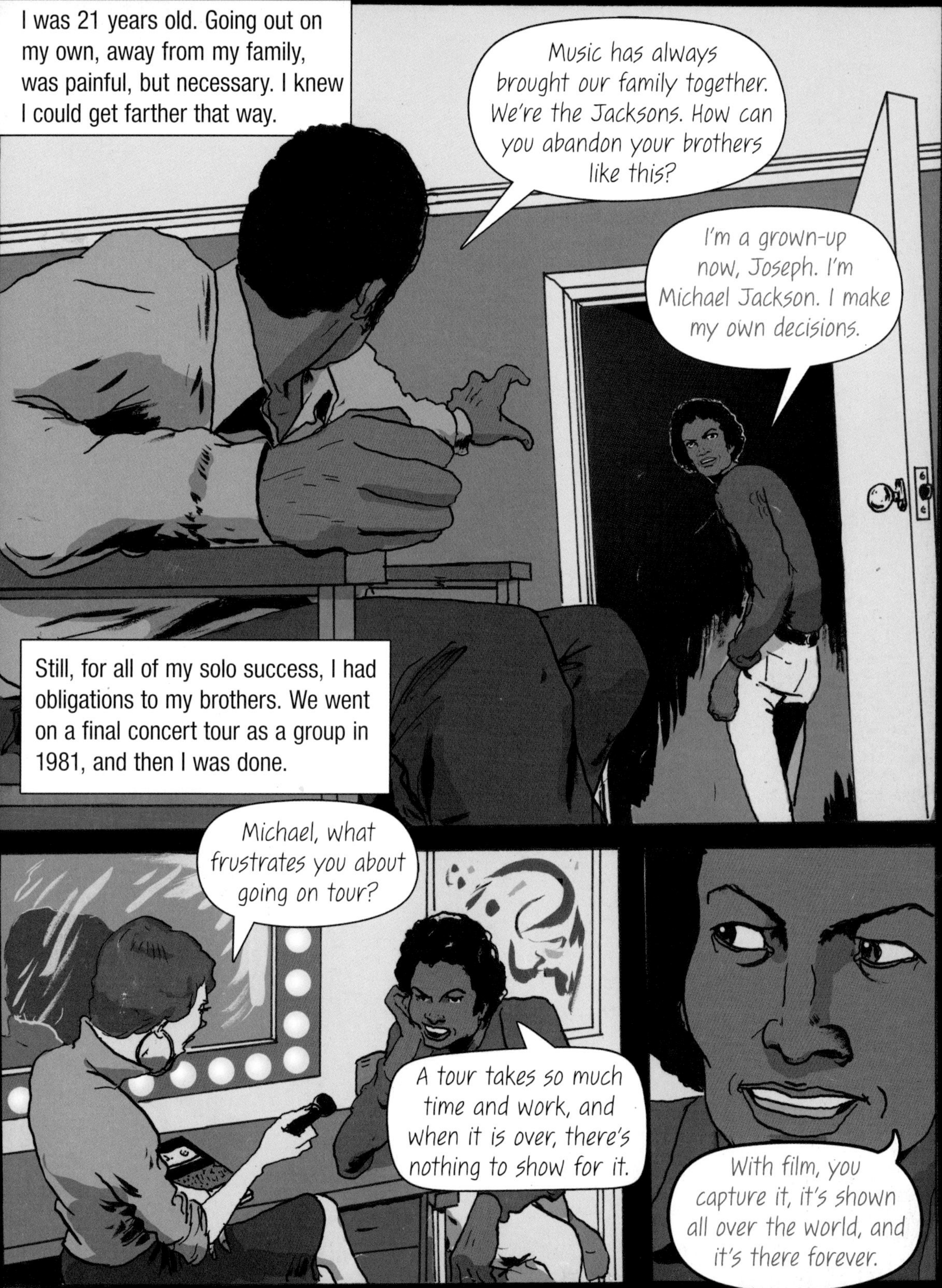

I was 21 years old. Going out on my own, away from my family, was painful, but necessary. I knew I could get farther that way.
Music has always brought our family together. We're the Jacksons. How can you abandon your brothers like this?
I'm a grown-up now, Joseph. I'm Michael Jackson. I make my own decisions.
Still, for all of my solo success, I had obligations to my brothers. We went on a final concert tour as a group in 1981, and then I was done.
Michael, what frustrates you about going on tour?
A tour takes so much time and work, and when it is over, there's nothing to show for it.
With film, you capture it, it's shown all over the world, and it's there forever.

Chapter 4
THRILLER

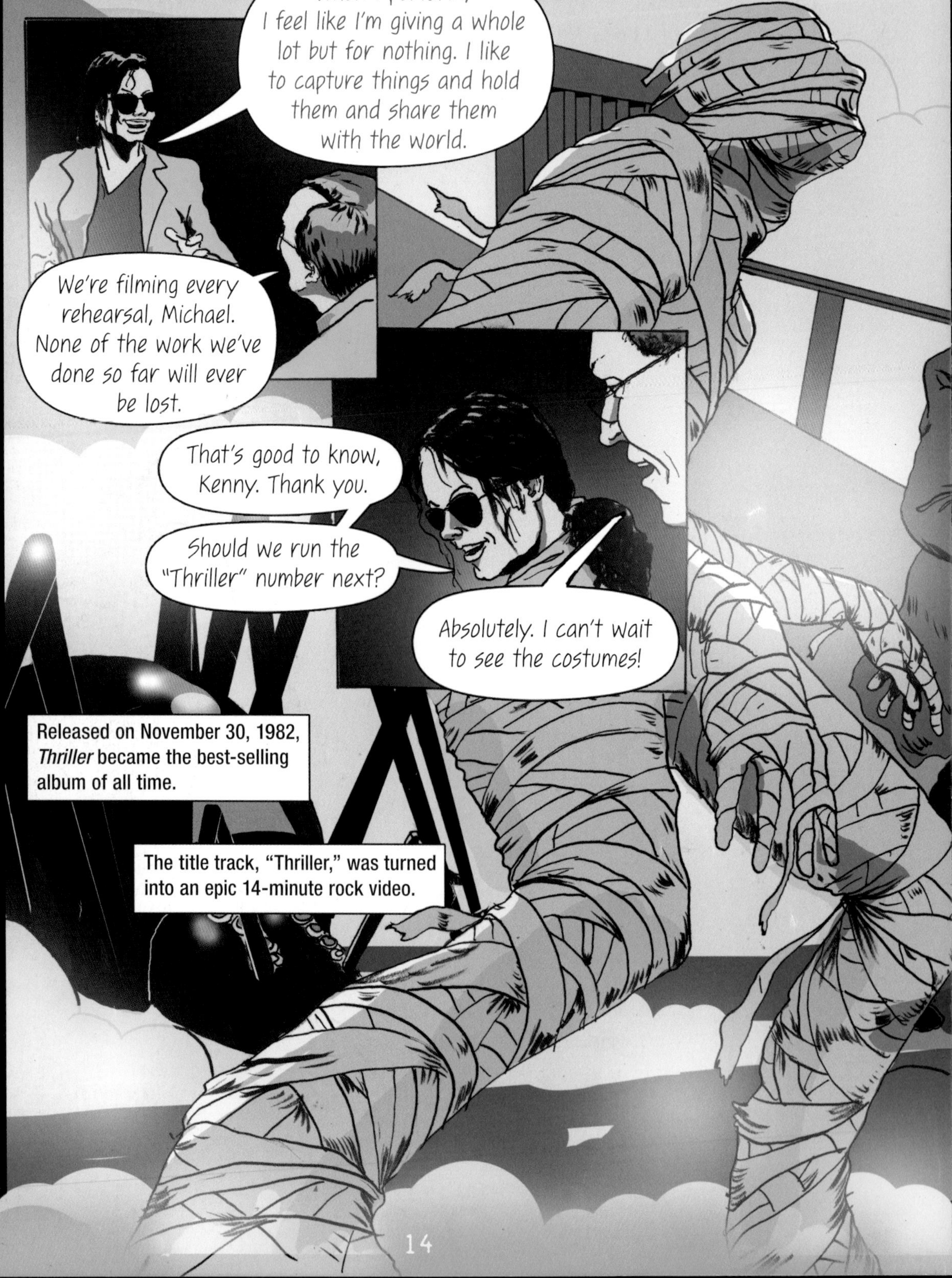

When I perform, I feel like I'm giving a whole lot but for nothing. I like to capture things and hold them and share them with the world.
We're filming every rehearsal, Michael. None of the work we've done so far will ever be lost.
That's good to know, Kenny. Thank you.
Should we run the "Thriller" number next?
Absolutely. I can't wait to see the costumes!
Released on November 30, 1982, *Thriller* became the best-selling album of all time.
The title track, "Thriller," was turned into an epic 14-minute rock video.

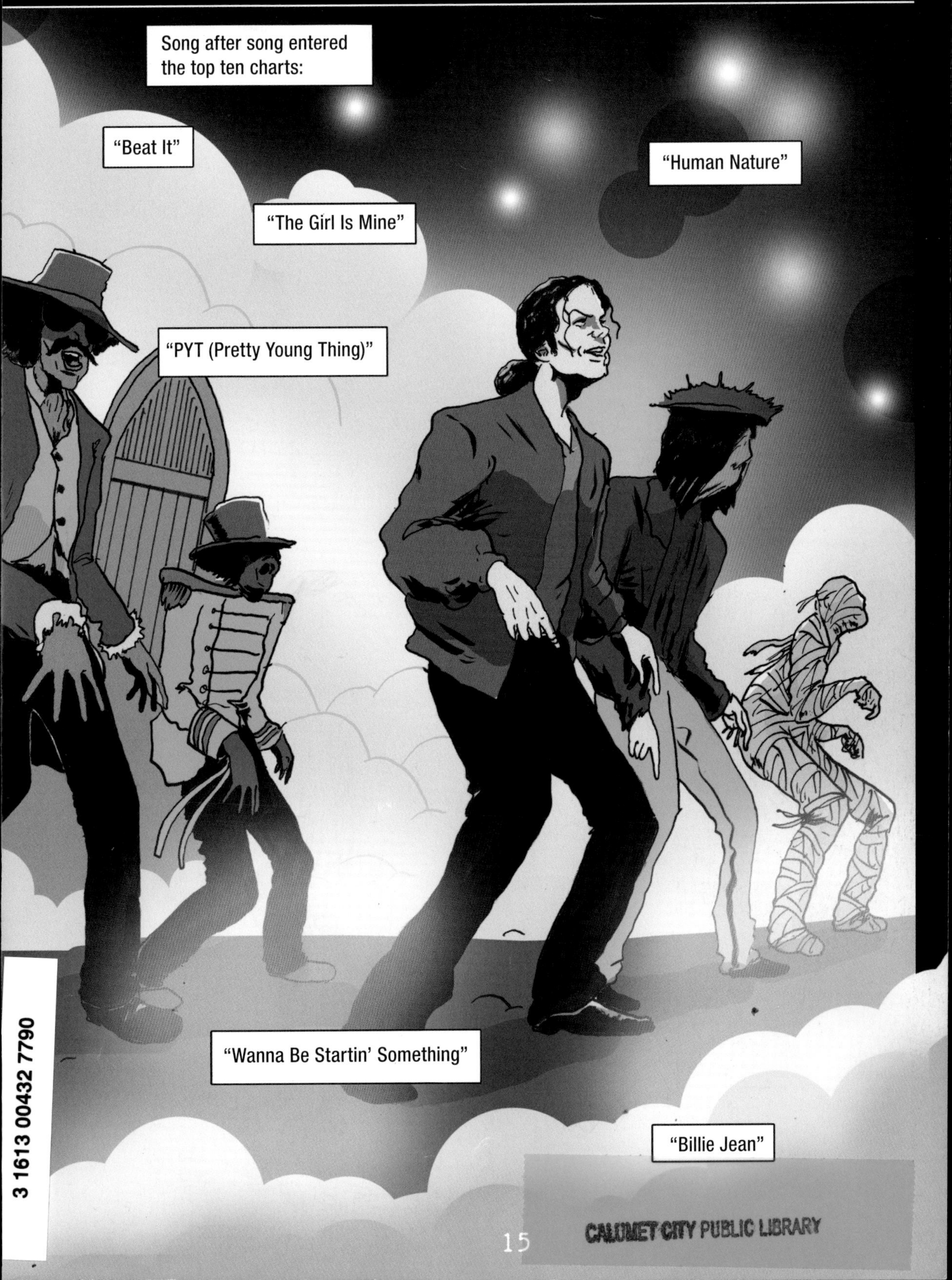
Song after song entered the top ten charts:
"Beat It"
"Human Nature"
"The Girl Is Mine"
"PYT (Pretty Young Thing)"
"Wanna Be Startin' Something"
"Billie Jean"

Chapter 5
BILLIE JEAN

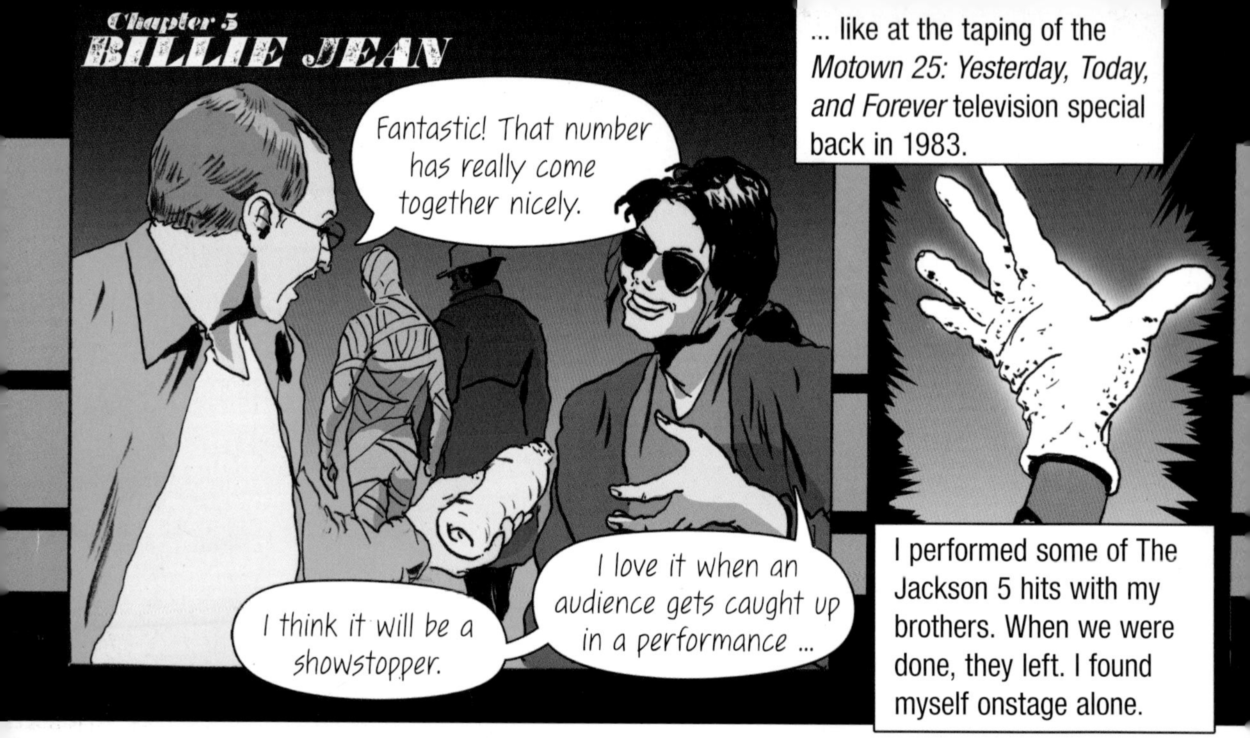

Fantastic! That number has really come together nicely.
I think it will be a showstopper.
I love it when an audience gets caught up in a performance ...
... like at the taping of the *Motown 25: Yesterday, Today, and Forever* television special back in 1983.
I performed some of The Jackson 5 hits with my brothers. When we were done, they left. I found myself onstage alone.

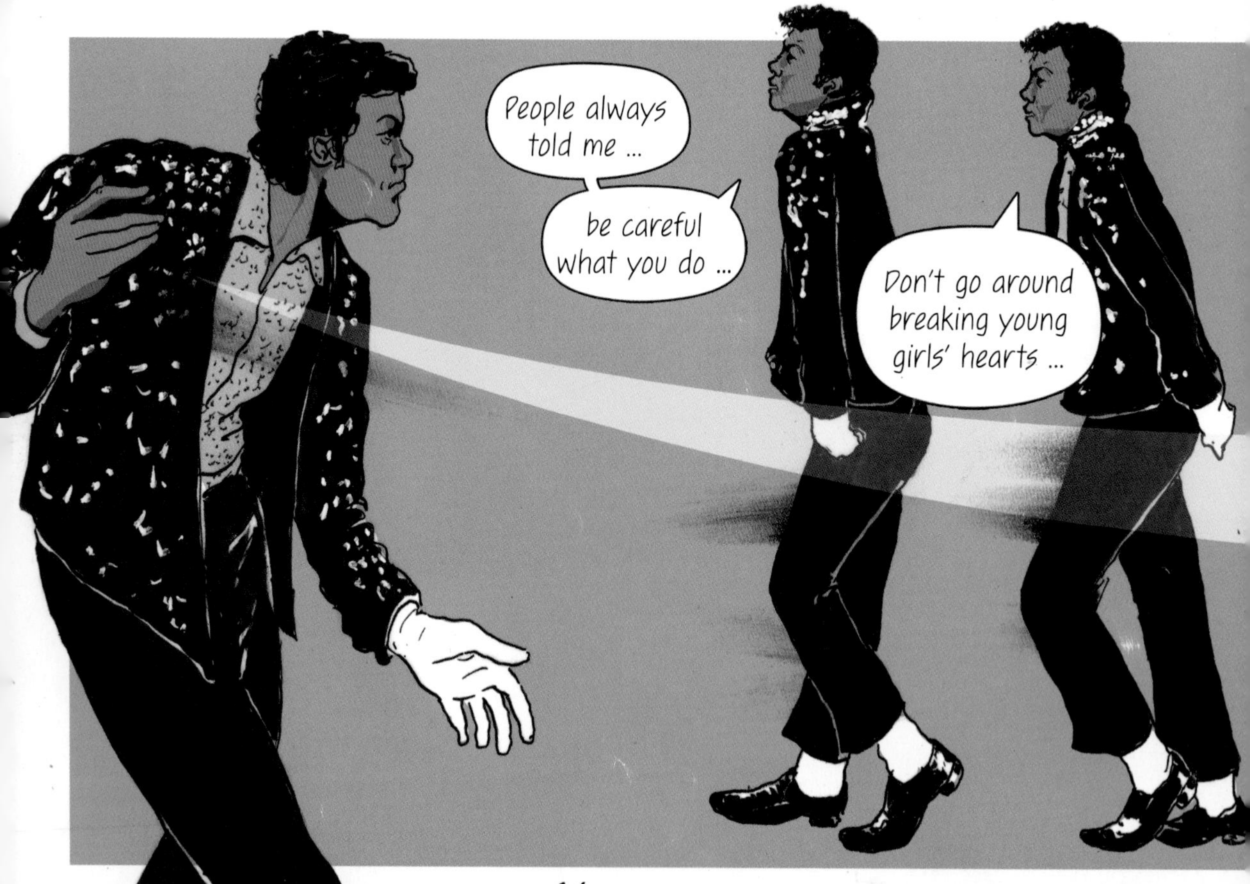

People always told me ...
be careful what you do ...
Don't go around breaking young girls' hearts ...

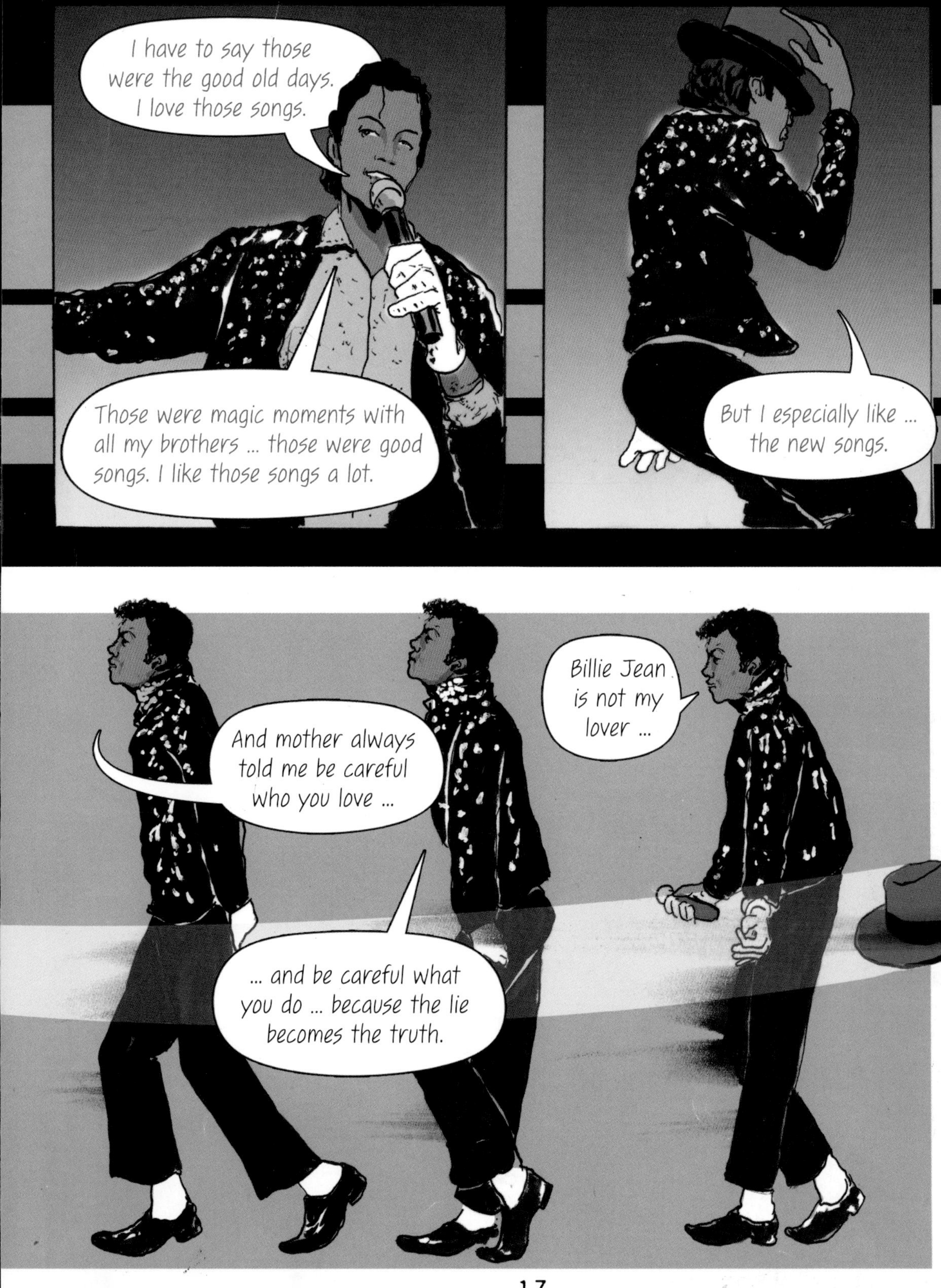
I have to say those were the good old days. I love those songs.
Those were magic moments with all my brothers ... those were good songs. I like those songs a lot.
But I especially like ... the new songs.
Billie Jean is not my lover ...
And mother always told me be careful who you love ...
... and be careful what you do ... because the lie becomes the truth.

Chapter 6
WE ARE THE WORLD

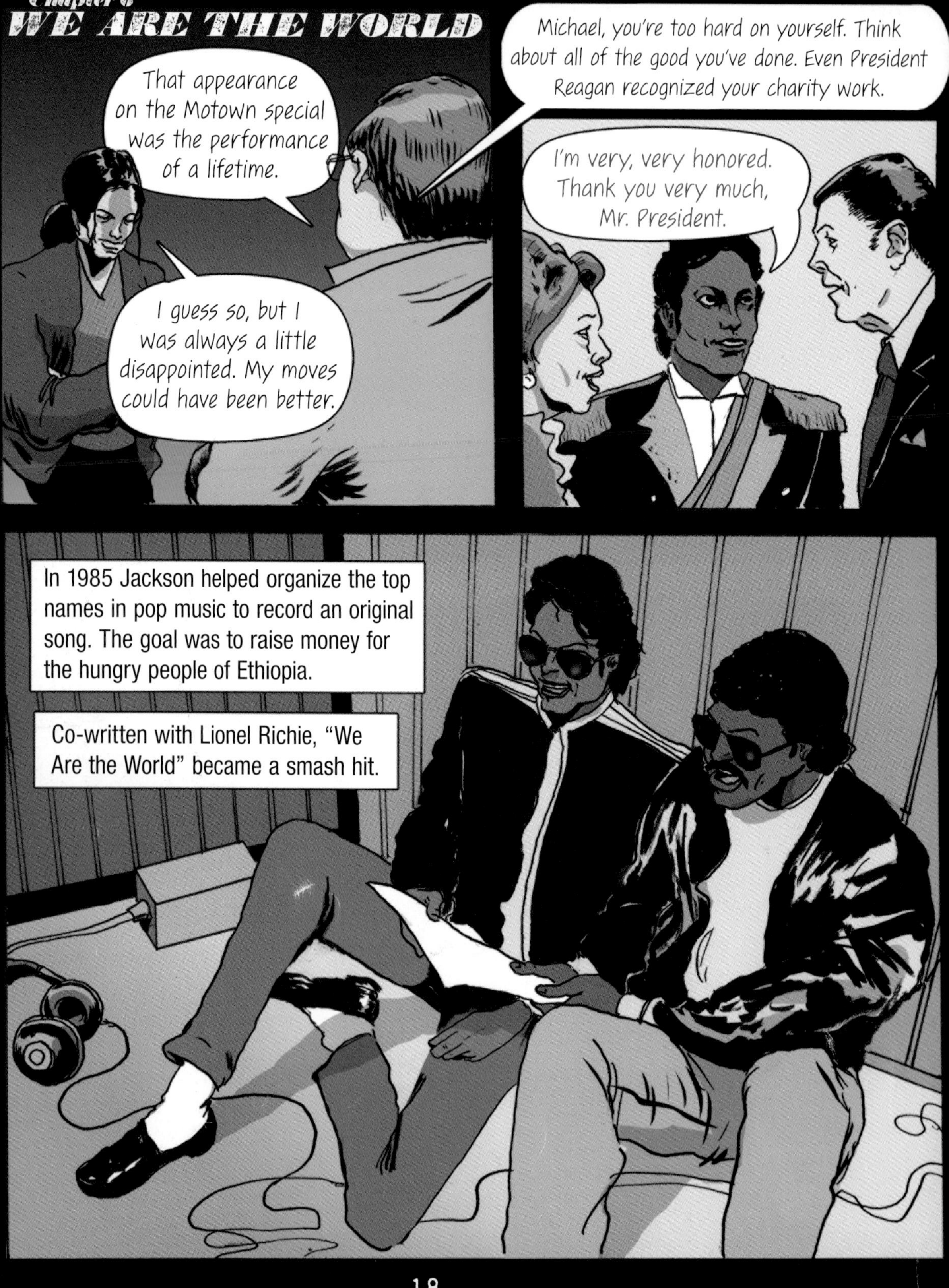
That appearance on the Motown special was the performance of a lifetime.
I guess so, but I was always a little disappointed. My moves could have been better.
Michael, you're too hard on yourself. Think about all of the good you've done. Even President Reagan recognized your charity work.
I'm very, very honored. Thank you very much, Mr. President.
In 1985 Jackson helped organize the top names in pop music to record an original song. The goal was to raise money for the hungry people of Ethiopia.
Co-written with Lionel Richie, "We Are the World" became a smash hit.

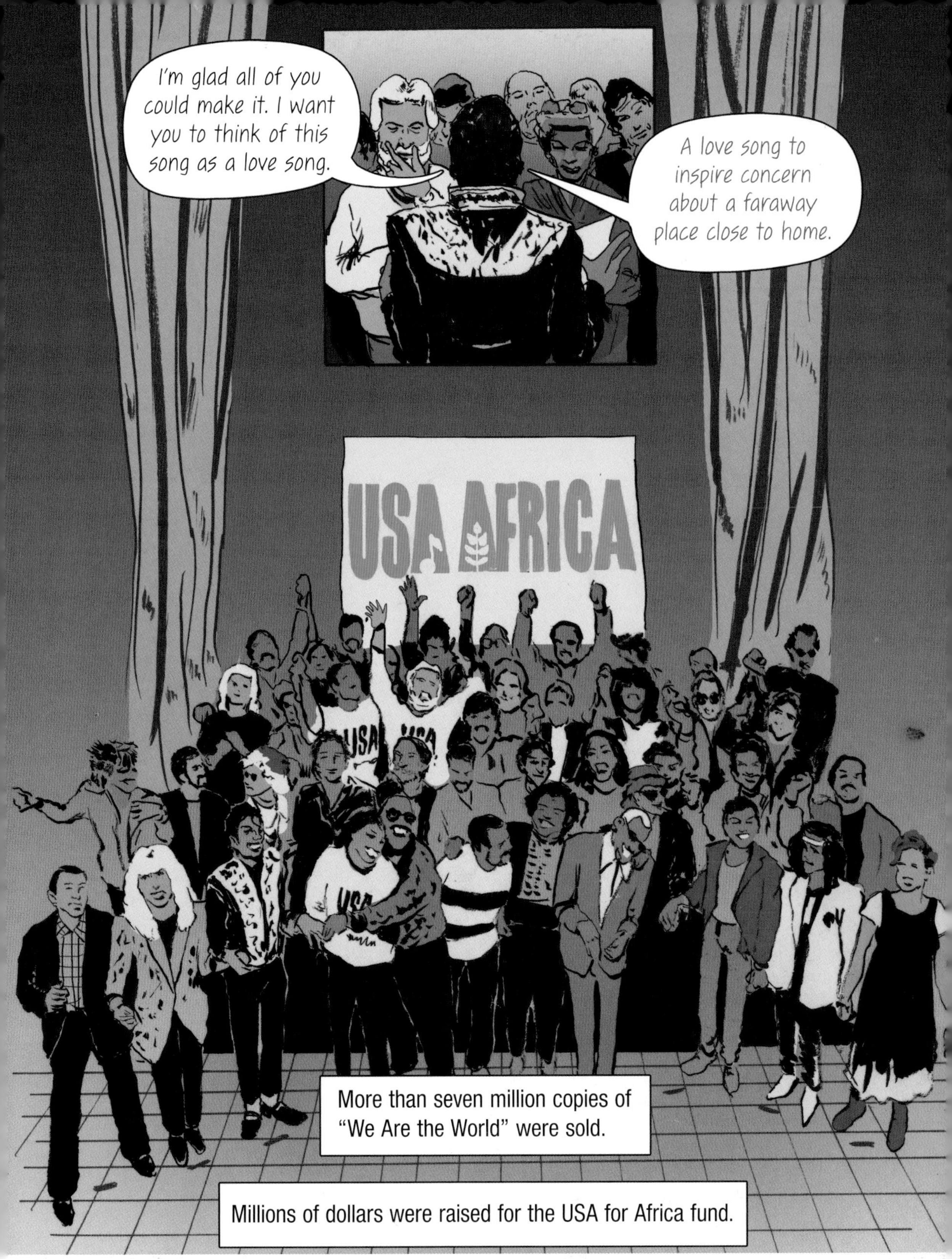
I'm glad all of you could make it. I want you to think of this song as a love song.
A love song to inspire concern about a faraway place close to home.
USA AFRICA
More than seven million copies of "We Are the World" were sold.
Millions of dollars were raised for the USA for Africa fund.

Chapter 7
LEAVE ME ALONE

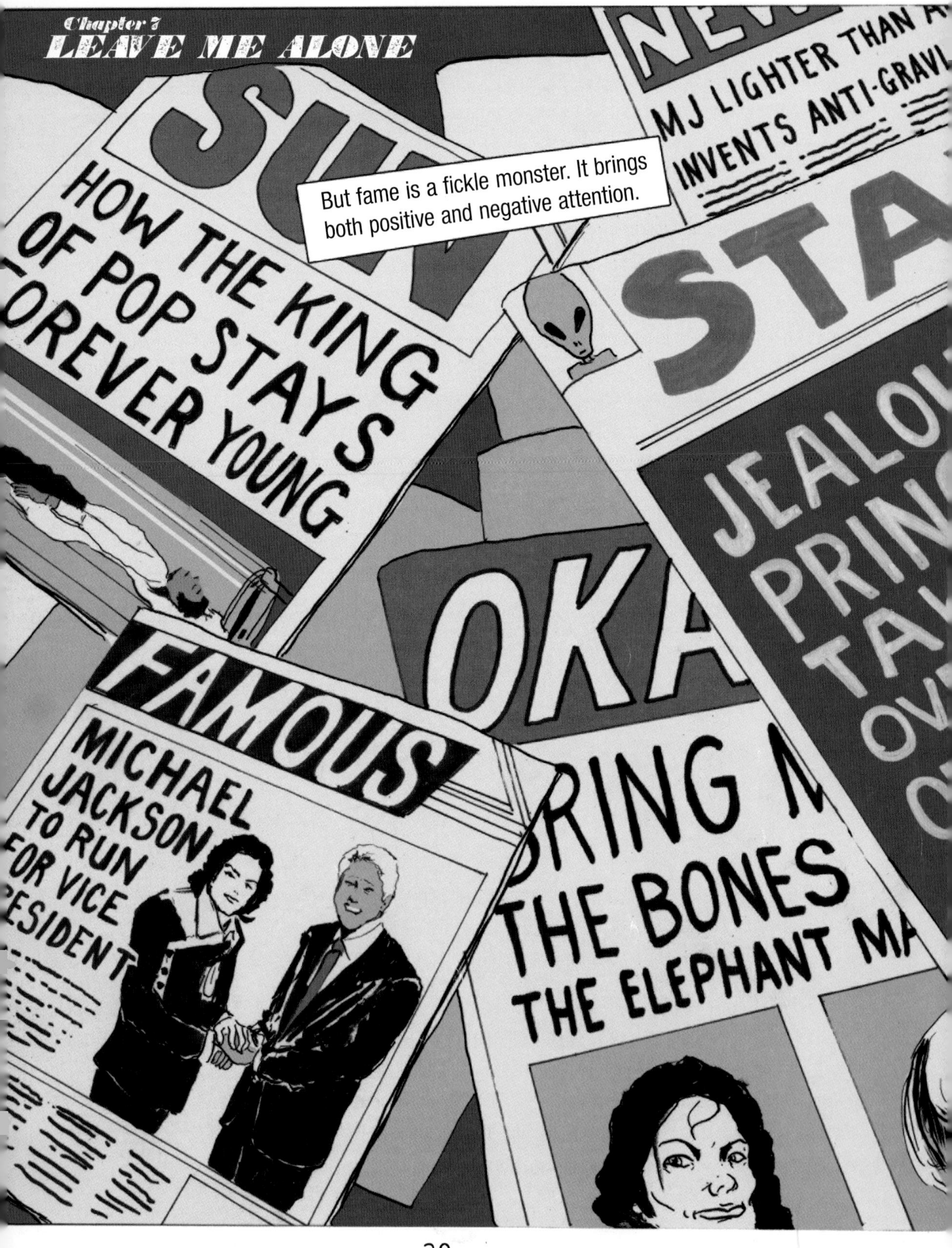
But fame is a fickle monster. It brings both positive and negative attention.
MJ LIGHTER THAN A
INVENTS ANTI-GRAV
HOW THE KING OF POP STAYS FOREVER YOUNG
STA
JEALO
PRIN
TA
OV
OKA
FAMOUS
MICHAEL JACKSON TO RUN FOR VICE PRESIDENT
RING M
THE BONES
THE ELEPHANT MA

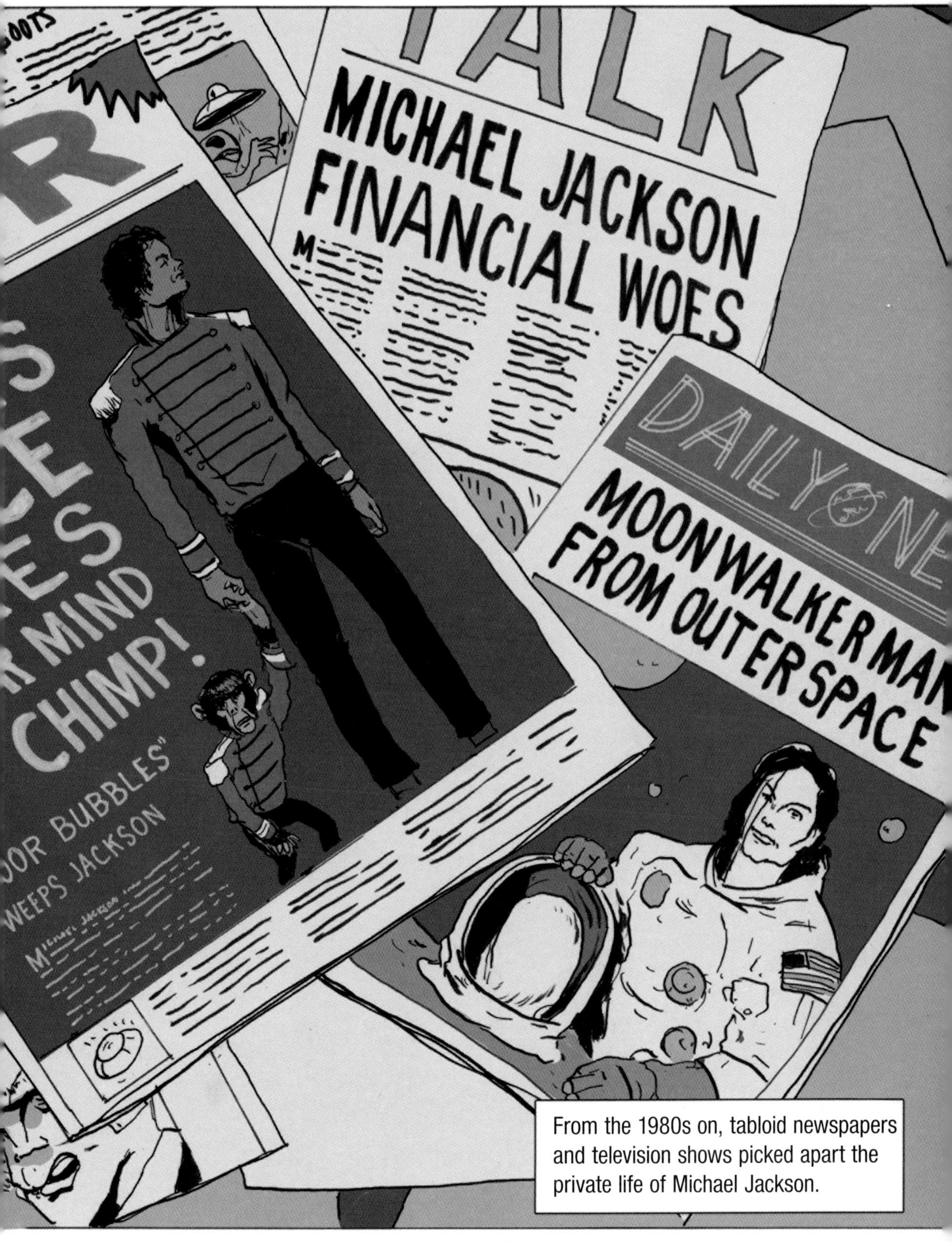
TALK
MICHAEL JACKSON FINANCIAL WOES
MOONWALKER MAN FROM OUTER SPACE
CHIMP!
BUBBLES"
JACKSON
From the 1980s on, tabloid newspapers and television shows picked apart the private life of Michael Jackson.

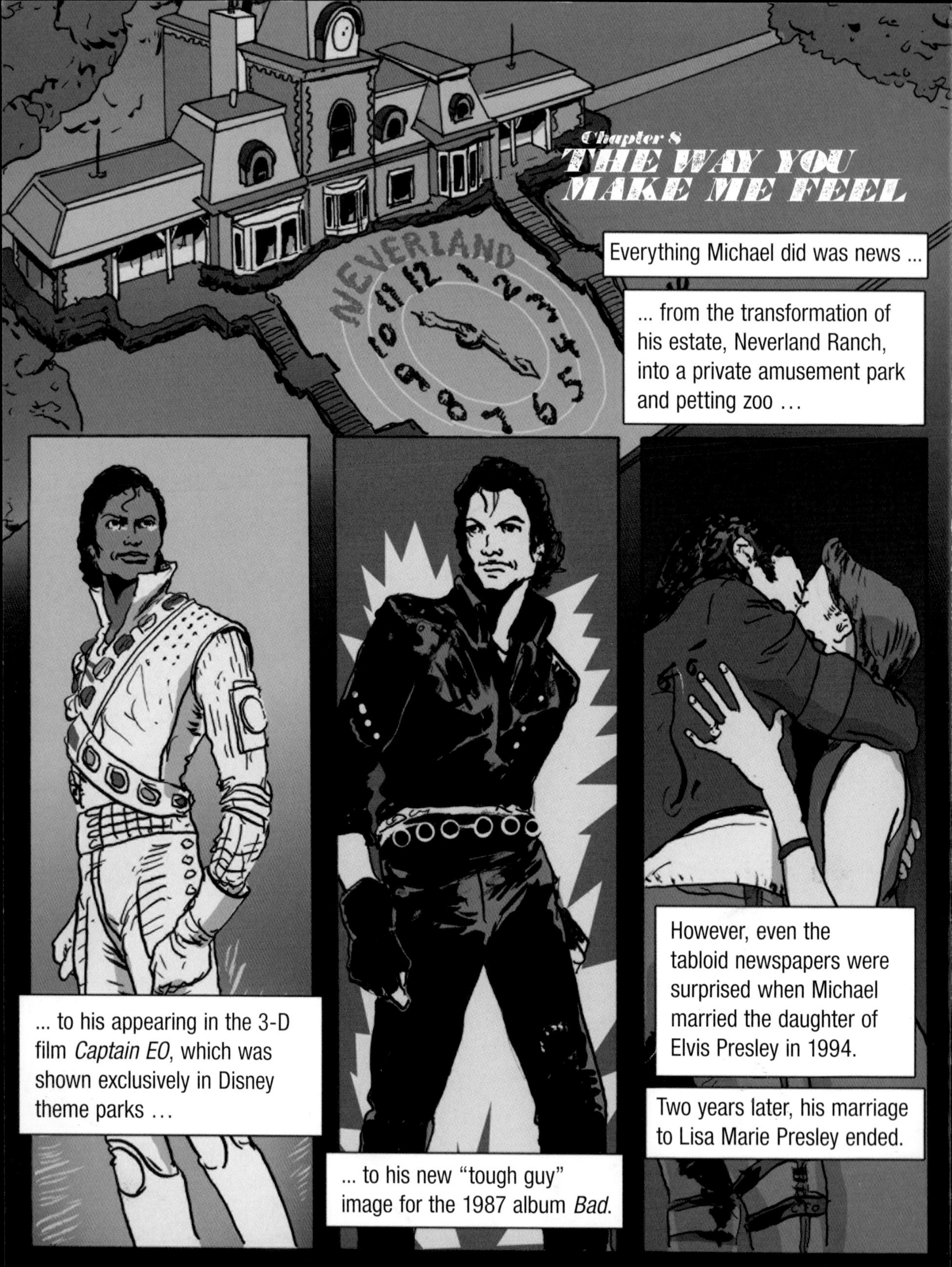
Chapter 8
THE WAY YOU MAKE ME FEEL
Everything Michael did was news ...
... from the transformation of his estate, Neverland Ranch, into a private amusement park and petting zoo ...
NEVERLAND
... to his appearing in the 3-D film *Captain EO*, which was shown exclusively in Disney theme parks ...
... to his new "tough guy" image for the 1987 album *Bad*.
However, even the tabloid newspapers were surprised when Michael married the daughter of Elvis Presley in 1994.
Two years later, his marriage to Lisa Marie Presley ended.

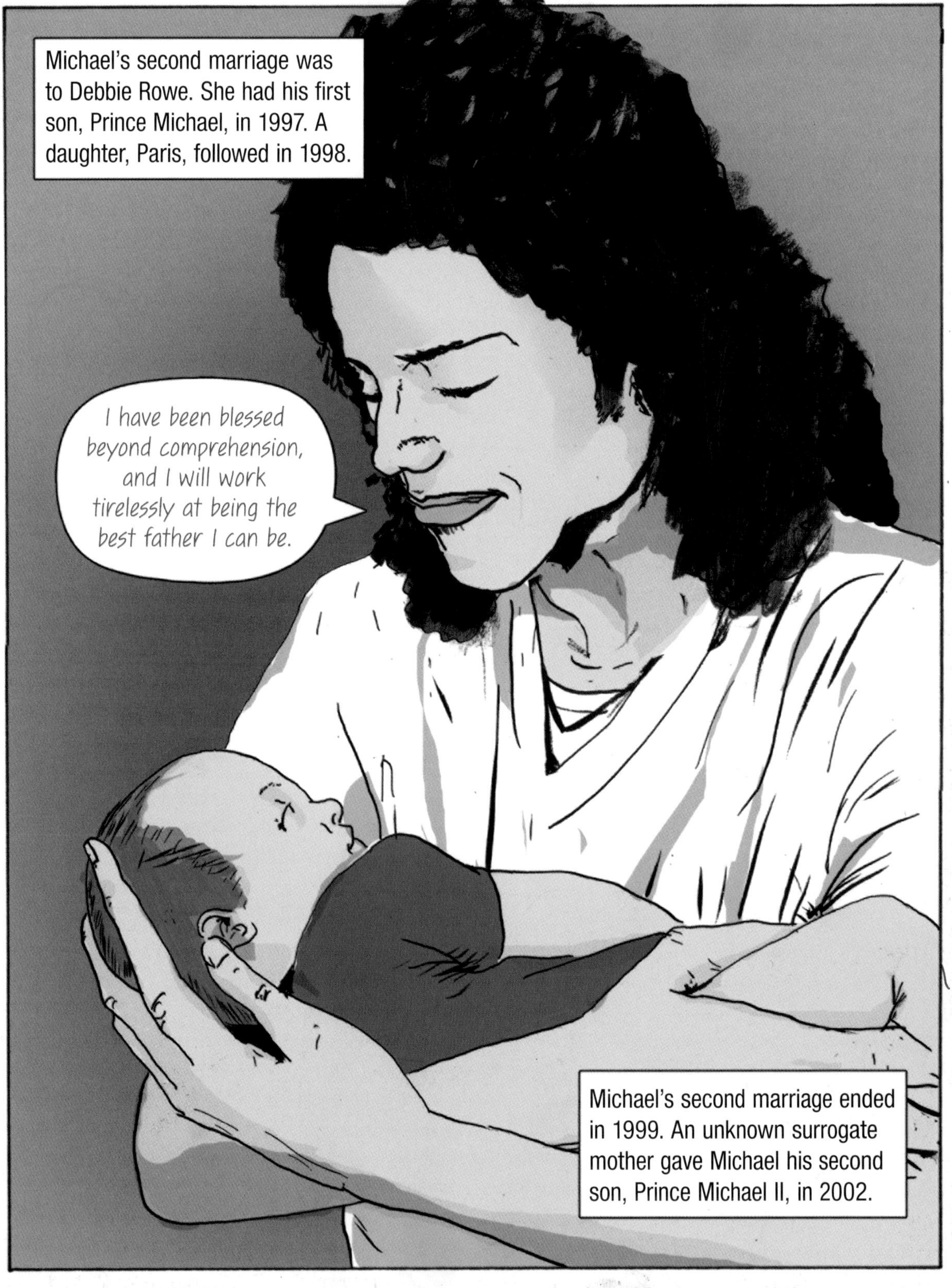
Michael's second marriage was to Debbie Rowe. She had his first son, Prince Michael, in 1997. A daughter, Paris, followed in 1998.
I have been blessed beyond comprehension, and I will work tirelessly at being the best father I can be.
Michael's second marriage ended in 1999. An unknown surrogate mother gave Michael his second son, Prince Michael II, in 2002.

Chapter 9
BLOOD ON THE DANCE FLOOR

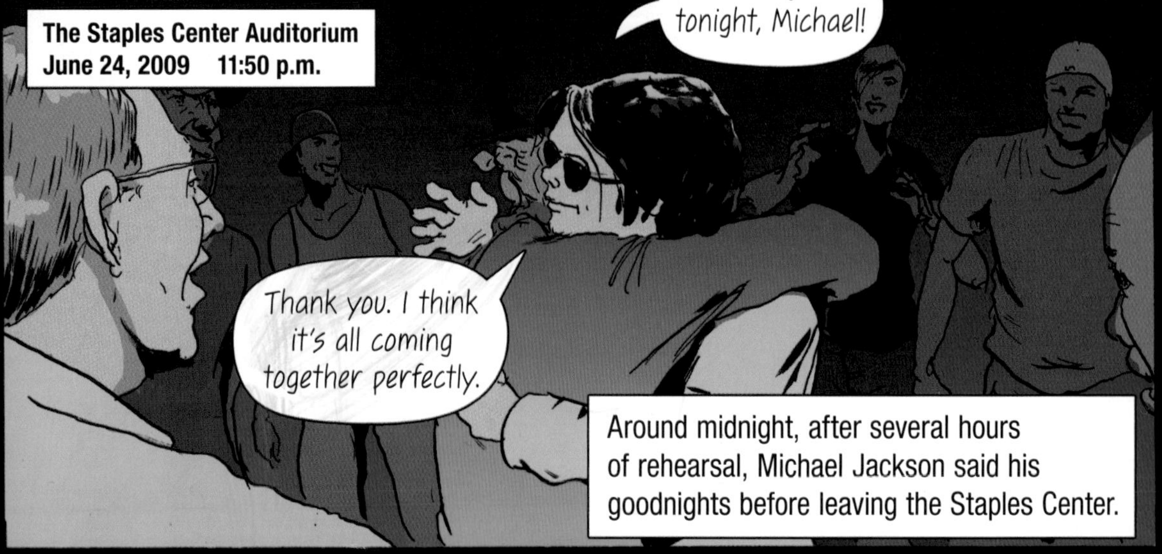
The Staples Center Auditorium
June 24, 2009 11:50 p.m.
Great job tonight, Michael!
Thank you. I think it's all coming together perfectly.
Around midnight, after several hours of rehearsal, Michael Jackson said his goodnights before leaving the Staples Center.

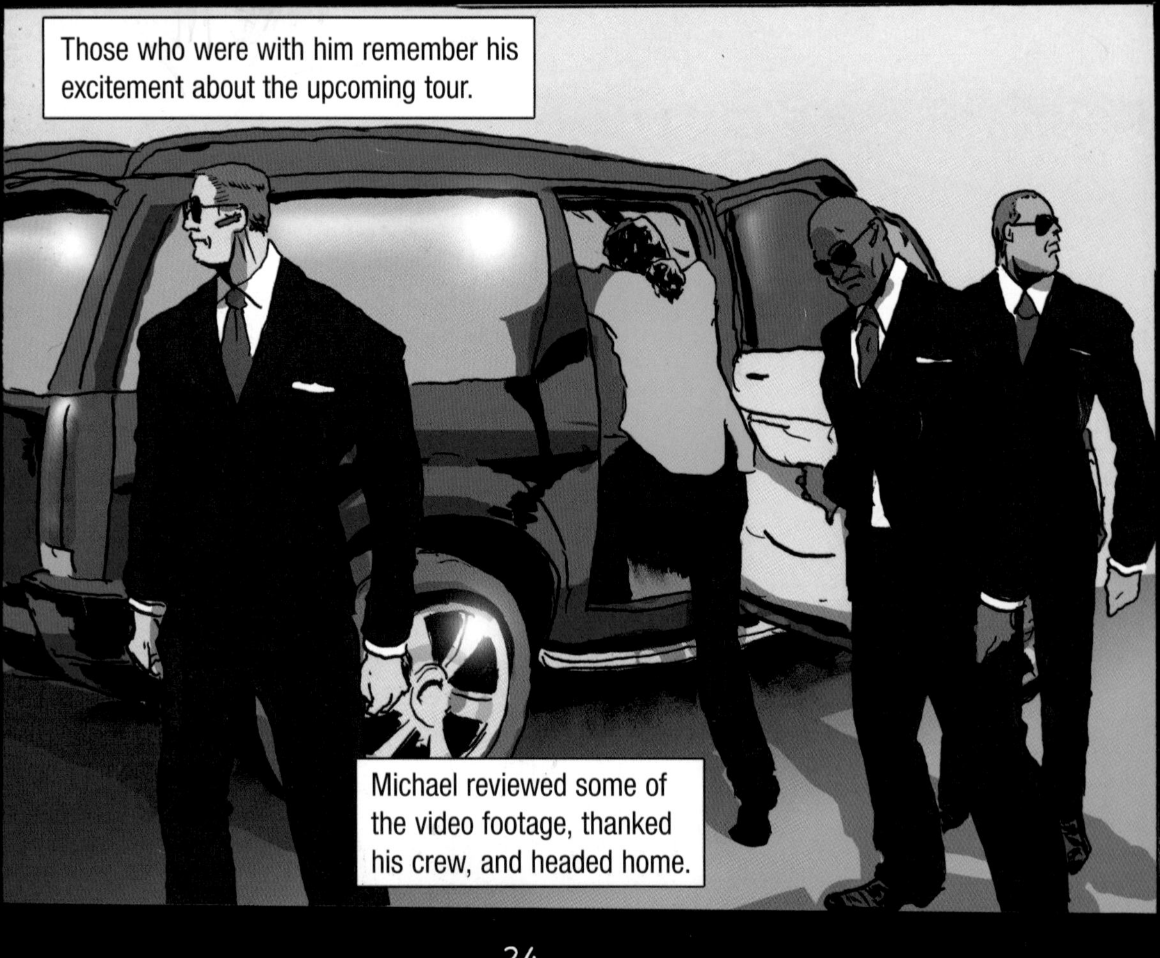
Those who were with him remember his excitement about the upcoming tour.
Michael reviewed some of the video footage, thanked his crew, and headed home.

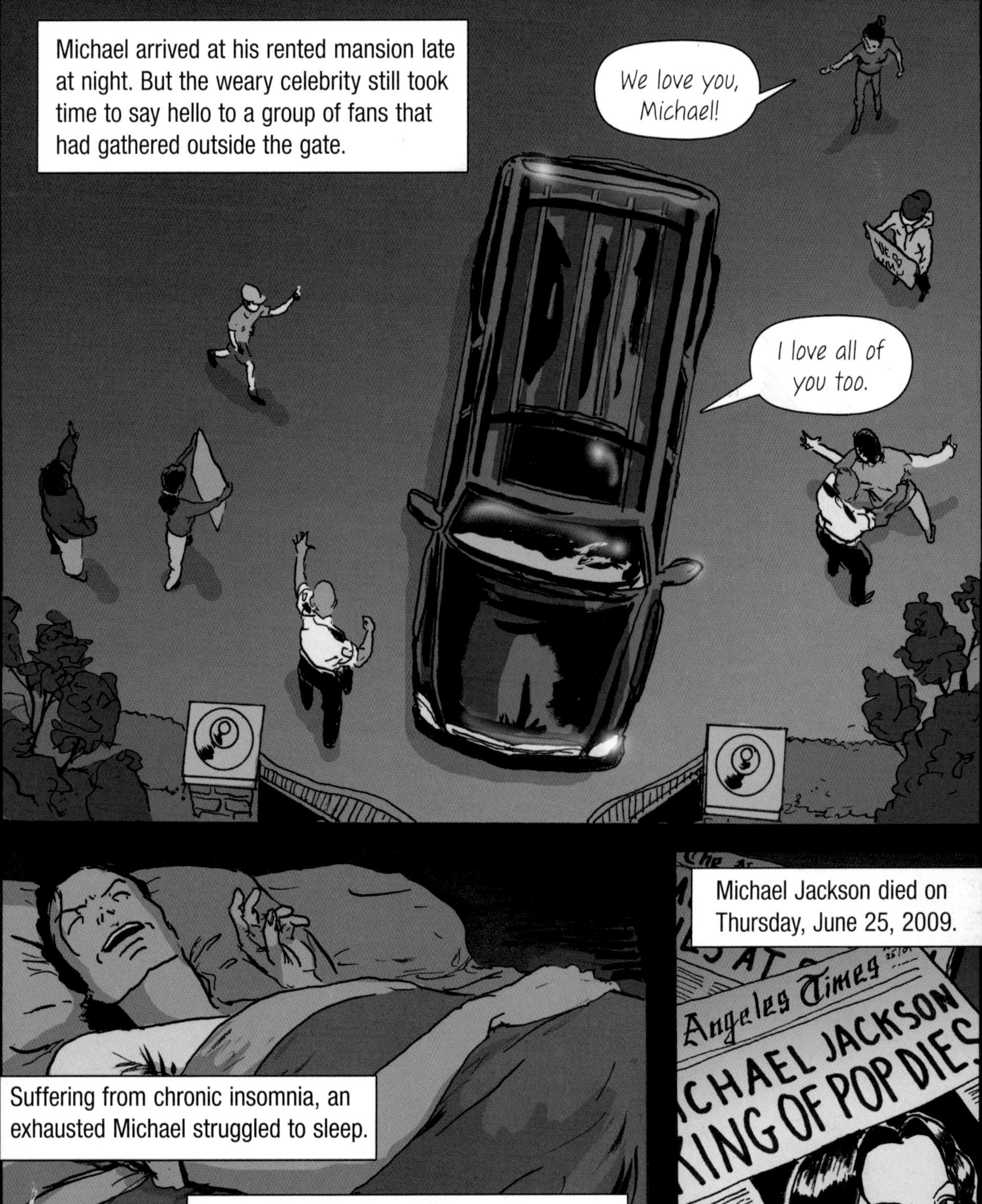
Michael arrived at his rented mansion late at night. But the weary celebrity still took time to say hello to a group of fans that had gathered outside the gate.
We love you, Michael!
I love all of you too.
Suffering from chronic insomnia, an exhausted Michael struggled to sleep.
The long night was restless and led into the dawn. Once he finally fell asleep, the King of Pop never awakened.
Michael Jackson died on Thursday, June 25, 2009.
Angeles Times
CHAEL JACKSON
ING OF POP DIES
Upon news of his death, the world mourned.

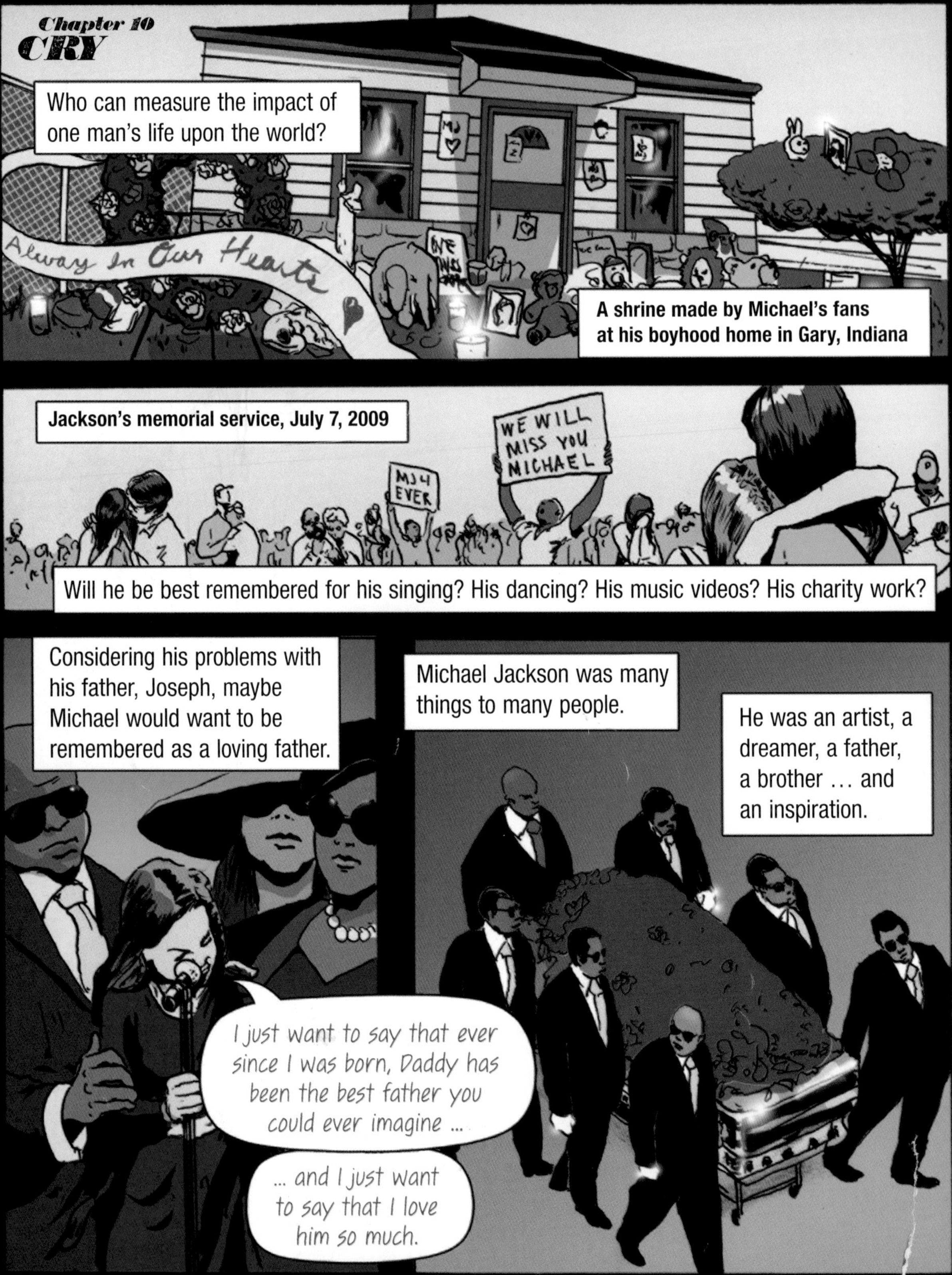
Chapter 10
CRY
Who can measure the impact of one man's life upon the world?
Always In Our Hearts
A shrine made by Michael's fans at his boyhood home in Gary, Indiana
Jackson's memorial service, July 7, 2009
MJ 4 EVER
WE WILL MISS YOU MICHAEL
Will he be best remembered for his singing? His dancing? His music videos? His charity work?
Considering his problems with his father, Joseph, maybe Michael would want to be remembered as a loving father.
I just want to say that ever since I was born, Daddy has been the best father you could ever imagine ...
... and I just want to say that I love him so much.
Michael Jackson was many things to many people.
He was an artist, a dreamer, a father, a brother ... and an inspiration.

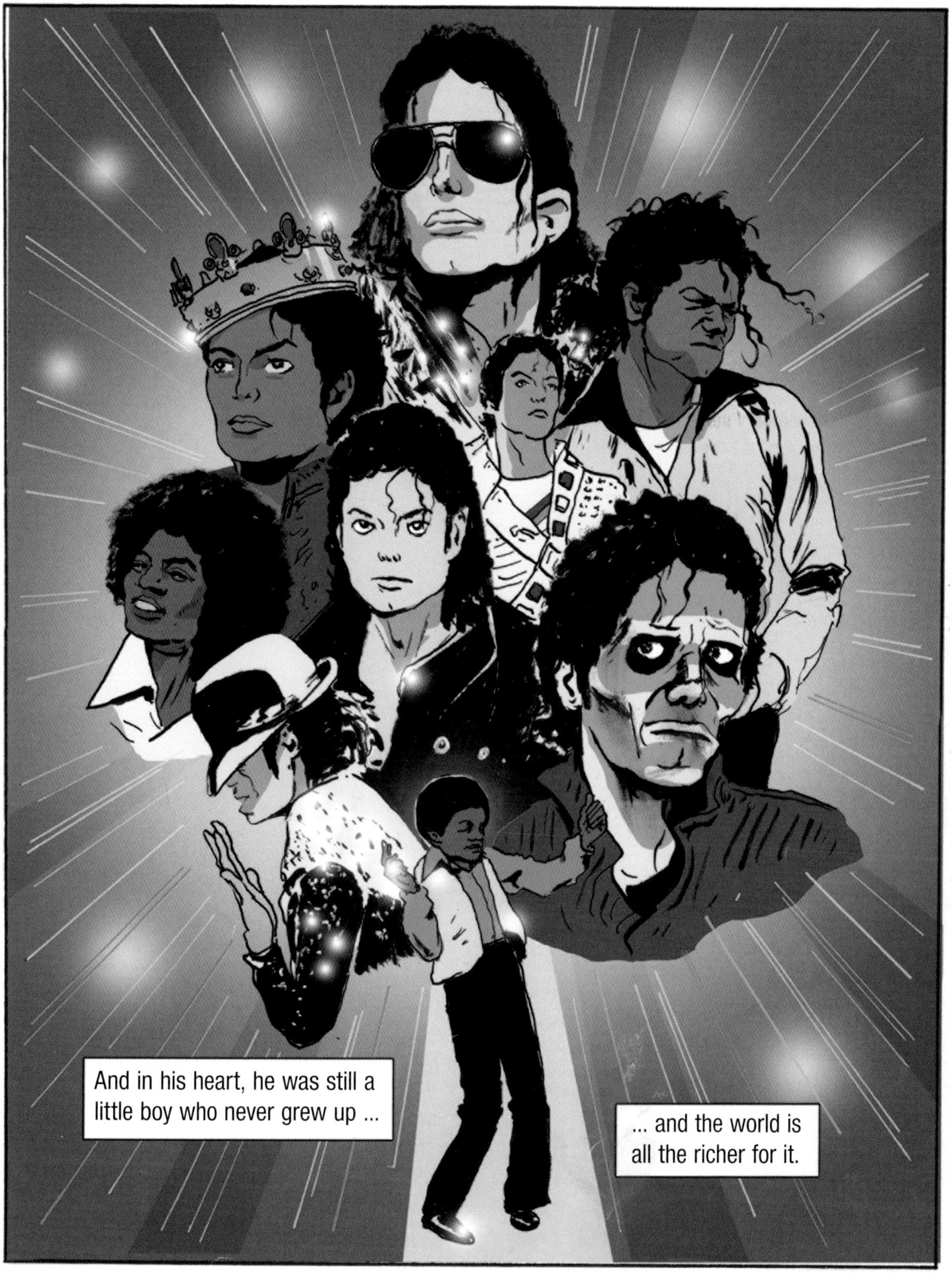
And in his heart, he was still a little boy who never grew up ...
... and the world is all the richer for it.

On June 25, 2009, the world lost a musical icon. No list of legendary musicians would be complete without the name Michael Jackson.

The Legacy of Michael

Michael Joseph Jackson was born in Gary, Indiana on August 29, 1958. He was the eighth of 10 children. Michael's father, Joseph Jackson, saw the musical talent in his children, and served as their manager. He was very strict and made them rehearse long hours, which often upset young Michael. But the hard work paid off. By 1968 the Jackson 5 signed a contract with Motown Records. Michael took the lead role in the group, guiding them to several number one records.

As Michael matured, he wanted to record music as a solo act. In 1979 he began managing his own career. Michael was not content to limit himself to one style of performing. He led the way as an artist with crossover appeal. His songs sold to all kinds of audiences, from fans of soul to rock to easy listening. Today, Michael is credited with inventing the category of "popular" music, hence his nickname, the King of Pop.

Unfortunately, along with the triumphs came heartbreak. Michael suffered from a fireworks accident in 1984 while filming a commercial. The accident resulted in second degree burns to his scalp. Corrective plastic surgery was needed to hide the scars. This was the first of many operations Michael underwent to change his appearance.

Michael was also a pioneer in making music into a theatrical performance. He was one of the first artists to create music videos. In 1982, with the release of his album *Thriller*, he became one of the best-selling recording artists of all time. Michael's videos combined his songs with striking images. These dynamic mini-movies showcased his trend-setting dance moves and one-of-a-kind fashion sense. His video performances were seen across the globe, making him a true international superstar. His dance moves and creative theatrical innovations continue to inspire today's artists.

Two short-lived marriages, the first of them to the daughter of rock legend Elvis Presley, ended in divorce. His odd behavior and colorful image sometimes overshadowed his music. In tabloid newspapers, Michael became known as "Wacko Jacko" for his eccentric lifestyle.

For several years, Michael stayed out of the public eye. He devoted himself to raising his kids and being the kind of father he had wanted as a child. However, approaching the age of 50, Michael decided to embark on a comeback tour. His unexpected death on June 25, 2009, shocked the world. An estimated one billion people around the world watched his televised memorial service.

GLOSSARY

album (AL-buhm)—a collection of music recorded on a CD, tape, or record

chronic (KRON-ik)—describes a problem that does not get better for a long time

critic (KRI-tik)—someone who reviews art, books, or movies

eccentric (ek-SEN-trik)—acting odd or strange, but in a harmless or charming way

fickle (FIK-uhl)—someone who is fickle changes his or her mind often

induct (in-DUHKT)—to formally admit someone into a position or place of honor

innovation (in-uh-VAY-shuhn)—a new idea or invention

insomnia (in-SOM-nee-uh)—not being able to fall asleep or stay asleep

mansion (MAN-shuhn)—a large and expensive house

mourn (MORN)—to be very sad and miss someone who has died

musical (MYOO-zuh-kuhl)—a show with singing and dancing

surrogate (SUR-uh-get)—a woman who carries a baby to term for another person to raise

tabloid (TAB-loid)—a newspaper that contains brief stories and pictures that are meant to stir up interest or cause excitement

READ MORE

Collins, Terry. *Elvis: A Graphic Novel.* American Graphic. Mankato, Minn.: Capstone Press, 2011.

Gunderson, Jessica. *Jay-Z: Hip-Hop Icon.* American Graphic. Mankato, Minn.: Capstone Press, 2012.

Krohn, Katherine. *Michael Jackson: Ultimate Music Legend.* Gateway Biographies. Minneapolis: Lerner, 2010.

INTERNET SITES

FactHound offers a safe, fun way to find Internet sites related to this book. All of the sites on FactHound have been researched by our staff.

Here's all you do:

Visit *www.facthound.com*

Type in this code: 9781429660150

Super-cool stuff! Check out projects, games and lots more at **www.capstonekids.com**

INDEX

AMERICAN GRAPHIC

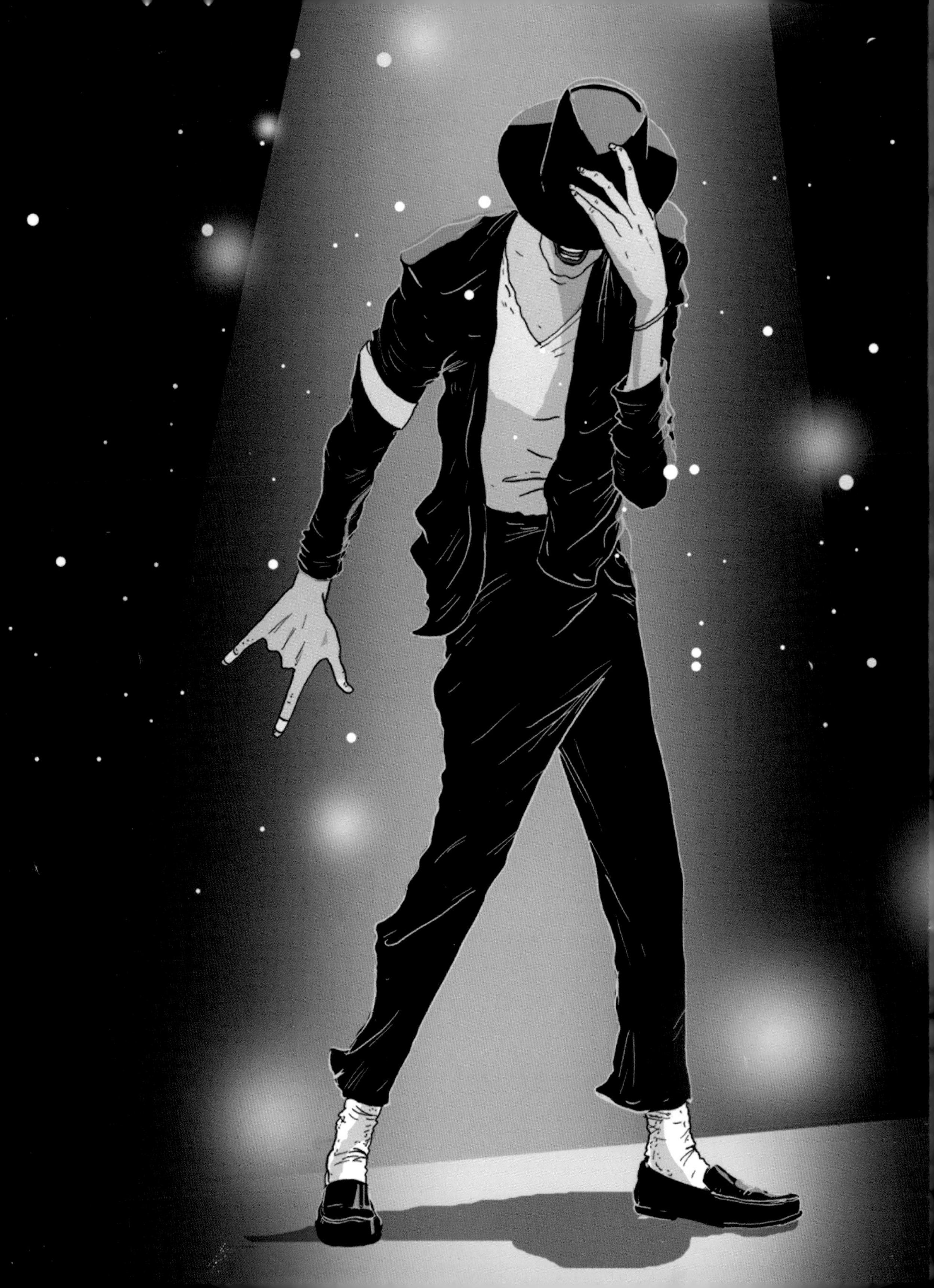